Endangered Species

by Russell Roberts

W9-CNA-239

OUR ENDANGERED PLANET

LUCENT Overview Series

Library of Congress Cataloging-in-Publication Data

Roberts, Russell, 1953–
        Endangered species / by Russell Roberts.
            p.   cm. — (Lucent overview series)
        Includes bibliographical references (p.   ) and index.
        Summary: Discusses various aspects of endangered species,
    including causes of extinction, land use, protection laws, and the
    race to prevent more extinctions.
        ISBN 1-56006-191-X (lib. bdg. : alk. paper)
        1. Endangered species—Juvenile literature.   2. Wildlife conser-
    vation—Juvenile literature.   3. Nature—Effect of human beings
    on—Juvenile literature.   [1. Endangered species.   2. Wildlife
    conservation.   3. Nature—Effect of human beings on.]   I. Title.
    II. Series.
    QL83.R63   1999
    333.95'22—dc21
                                                              98-15038
                                                                  CIP
                                                                   AC

No part of this book may be reproduced or used in any form or by any means, electrical,
mechanical, or otherwise, including, but not limited to, photocopy, recording, or any information storage and retrieval system, without prior written permission from the publisher.

Copyright © 1999 by Lucent Books, Inc.
P.O. Box 289011, San Diego, CA 92198-9011
Printed in the U.S.A.

Contents

Introduction

IN BRAZIL, FARMERS clearing land for planting crops are destroying the habitat of the golden lion tamarin, a South American monkey, driving it to the edge of extinction. In India, poachers ruthlessly hunt the endangered snow leopard for its thick coat because they can earn more in one week from selling the pelt than they can from months of farming. In Southeast Asia, the development of once deserted coastal areas into tourist beaches has significantly eroded the habitat of the Mediterranean monk seal, reducing the number of animals left in the world to just a few hundred.

Scenarios such as these are occurring every day around the world: People's needs clash with the needs of other species. Almost inevitably, when these clashes occur, the nonhuman species is the loser, often reduced so greatly in number that it becomes endangered. Sometimes, it even becomes extinct.

Conflicting rights

The pressures human activities place on species around the world increase daily. Pollution, development, the spread of agriculture, and the introduction of plants and animals into foreign environments are just some of the ways that people are putting more stress on a species' ability to survive.

Governments have tried to aid species by passing laws, preserving habitat areas in their natural states, banning or restricting hunting, and taking other protective measures.

But these steps often produce controversy and resentment. A poverty-stricken resident of the Third World will sell an endangered species to put food on the table for his family. To him, making it illegal to hunt a species is putting the species' rights above the rights of people.

Efforts to protect species have also run into trouble in industrialized countries. The Endangered Species Act (ESA) in the United States has prevented development,

Laws meant to protect endangered species, like this African elephant, often conflict with the rights of humans who share their habitat.

interfered with private property rights, and destroyed livelihoods. Yet without the safeguards that this law provides, it is likely that many more species would be added to the list of those that have become extinct. Trying to decide between the rights of species and the rights of humans has become one of the great balancing acts of modern times in many nations.

From mammals to fungi

What makes these decisions even more difficult is the scope of the problem. A species is a natural biological group that shares a common pool of genes. Thus the term *species* applies to everything from animals to insects and even fungi. Although people often associate the phrase *endangered species* only with large mammals, such as elephants, tigers, or whales, in reality there are many, many species that are struggling to survive. Attempting to preserve all of these species has become a monumental problem.

To some people, the problem is simple: Save those species that are "popular," i.e., mammals, and don't worry about those that aren't, such as insects. Yet, using people's attachment to certain animals ignores other criteria that may be even more important to the human species. Imagine, for example, that an insect that was allowed to become extinct carried the cure for all known forms of cancer in its genetic makeup. Were such a discovery made, popularity would be a less important criterion for which species to save.

This dilemma encompasses the issue of endangered species. It is a dilemma that seems to produce no answers, only more questions. The resolution of this dilemma will have profound consequences for both endangered species and humanity.

1

Laws That Protect Endangered Species

LAWS AND TREATIES are two powerful tools that nations throughout the world use to try to provide legal protection for endangered and threatened species. Unfortunately, though well intentioned, these efforts have sometimes fallen short of their goal.

The Endangered Species Act

The Endangered Species Act (ESA) was passed by the U.S. Congress and signed into law by President Richard M. Nixon on December 28, 1973. This comprehensive law provided legal protection for endangered species and gave the federal government broad powers to prevent the destruction of species and their habitat.

The ESA established three categories to describe the status of a given species: endangered, threatened, and stable.

A species is classified as endangered when it is in imminent danger of extinction throughout all or a significant portion of its range (the area in which it lives). A species is considered threatened when it is likely to become endangered within the foreseeable future. A stable species is one that is neither endangered nor threatened.

The ESA covers all species, including fish, birds, insects (except those considered pests), plants, fungi, and every other living organism. While the main focus of the ESA is on U.S. domestic species, it also attempts to prevent the exploitation of endangered species in other countries by

9

© Engleman/Rothco. Used with permission.

ROTHCO
ORIGINAL

ENGLEMAN.

"CHIEF, WE'VE LOCATED BIG FOOT AND I'M AFRAID
HE'S NOT AS DUMB AS WE THOUGHT!"

banning the importation of and trade in any product derived from these species.

The Fish and Wildlife Service (FWS), a bureau of the
U.S. Department of the Interior, is the primary enforcer of
the ESA. It maintains a list of endangered and threatened
species in the United States and other countries. FWS depends on official and unofficial reports, petitions, and research findings to learn about species that may be eligible
for the list. Any person or organization can nominate a
species for the list.

Once a species has been proposed for the list, FWS con-
ducts an investigation. Depending on the results, the agency will either list the species or deny the nomination.

As of March 31, 1998, 1,134 animal and plant species
within the United States were on the endangered and

threatened list. Of this total, 902 were endangered (349 animals, 553 plants) and 232 were threatened (117 animals, 115 plants). When foreign species were included, the total rose to 1,694.

In keeping with the ultimate goals of the ESA, the FWS is responsible for developing recovery plans that will help the population of each species increase to a point at which it is no longer in danger of extinction, and can be removed from the list.

The ESA also requires the FWS to conserve and protect "the ecosystems upon which endangered and threatened species of wildlife depend." Thus, the FWS is also responsible for habitat protection.

In addition, the ESA prohibits "taking" an endangered species. The law defines taking as harassing, harming, pursuing, hunting, shooting, wounding, trapping, killing,

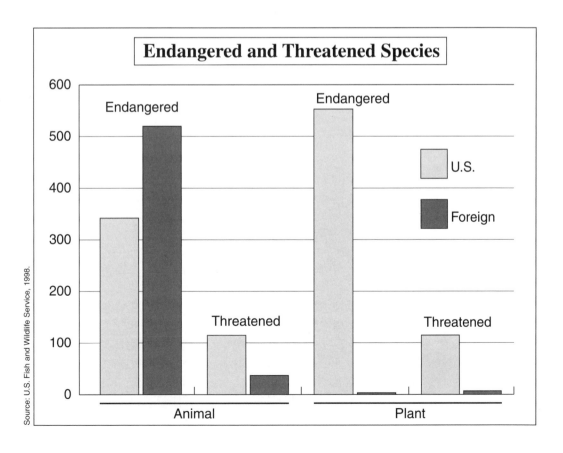

Source: U.S. Fish and Wildlife Service, 1998.

capturing, or collecting the species. The law gives FWS the authority to stop any activity, whether on public or private land, that constitutes "taking" an endangered species or disturbing its habitat. This means that the federal government can halt any private, commercial, or industrial activity that threatens a species or its habitat, from the construction of a gigantic dam to the plow of a single farmer. It is this provision of the law that has generated a great deal of controversy.

Has the ESA been effective?

Determining the effectiveness of the ESA is difficult. The law has only been in effect since 1973, while the forces endangering species have been operating for generations.

Critics argue that the best way to measure the law's success is to determine how many species have been declared "recovered" and removed from the list. Unfortunately, by this criteria the ESA has failed.

From the end of 1973 to the end of 1993, 721 species were added to the endangered and threatened list. During this same period, just 21 species were removed. This means that additions outnumbered removals by approximately 34 to 1.

The gray whale was taken off the ESA's endangered and threatened species list in 1994. Critics maintain that this is not a success story for the ESA because the gray whale's numbers were recovering long before it was listed.

Furthermore, not all of the species were removed because they recovered. Some became extinct; others were listed before the discovery of additional populations qualified them for removal.

Even the few successes claimed since ESA enactment have been criticized. For example, the gray whale was delisted in 1994 because its population had rebounded. However, according to Robert E. Gordon, executive director of the National Wilderness Institute, the number of whales has been growing since 1890—long before the ESA existed.

Another species that conservationists claim has recovered under the ESA is the bald eagle. Because its numbers have risen over the last two decades, in 1994 the bald eagle was reclassified from endangered to threatened in all but three of the lower forty-eight states. However, Gordon claims that it was the 1972 ban on the pesticide DDT, highly toxic to birds, that led to the eagle's recovery, not ESA restrictions.

Supporters of the ESA claim that the bald eagle's status has improved from endangered to threatened under its restrictions.

Supporters of the ESA argue its effectiveness. Michael J. Bean, chairperson of the Environmental Defense Fund's Wildlife Program, agrees that the DDT ban has indeed helped the eagle. However, he points out that ESA-mandated restrictions on hunting and habitat destruction have also played a significant role in helping the raptors recover.

Bean cites a number of species that he believes have benefited from the ESA: Populations of the whooping crane, California sea otter, peregrine falcon, brown pelican, red wolf, black-footed ferret, and Columbia white-tailed deer have all increased under the law's protection.

Has the Endangered Species Act been effective? Its supporters concede that they would have liked to see more species declared recovered, but contend that although it isn't perfect, if the ESA were abandoned, it might result in even more endangered species.

The Marine Mammal Protection Act

The Marine Mammal Protection Act (MMPA) is another U.S. law that safeguards species. Enacted in 1972, the MMPA protects and manages marine mammals and their products, such as the processing of parts, such as fur or whalebone, and consumption of meat. It established a moratorium, with certain exceptions, on the taking of marine mammals in U.S. waters and by U.S. citizens on the high seas. It also banned the importation into the United States of marine mammals and products made from these animals. Among the species covered by the MMPA are polar bears, walruses, sea otters, sea lions, whales, seals, and porpoises.

CITES

The Convention on International Trade in Endangered Species of Wild Fauna and Flora, or CITES (pronounced SY-teez), is an international treaty that regulates the trade in endangered flora and fauna. It was conceived in 1973 by the International Union for the Conservation of Nature and Natural Resources (IUCN), and is currently administered from Geneva, Switzerland, by the United Nations Environmental Programme (UNEP). Over 130 nations have ratified CITES, making it the most widely supported treaty of any kind in the world.

CITES is designed to act like an international traffic signal: It halts trade in some species that are endangered and urges caution for others that could become endangered without the proper precautions. The convention monitors and regulates trade in over forty thousand species of plants and animals through a permit system. Permits to hunt or harvest a species are issued only if member nations are satisfied that the survival of the species is not at risk. Traffickers must report totals to CITES offices, which record and analyze figures to make sure that healthy populations are maintained. The use of special paper and stamps helps prevent these permits from being forged.

CITES classifies species under one of two headings: Appendix I lists critically endangered species, Appendix II those at serious risk.

Species listed under Appendix I include all apes, lemurs, many South American monkeys, the giant panda, great whales, cheetahs, leopards, tigers, elephants, rhinos, parrots, sea turtles, and giant salamanders.

Appendix II species include primates and tortoises not already listed in Appendix I, as well as dolphins, porpoises, orchids, birds of prey, some snails, fur seals, and numerous other species.

Every two and one-half years, representatives of CITES member nations meet in a different city to evaluate the status of the species covered by the treaty.

Has CITES been effective?

CITES suffers from a lack of enforcement capabilities, a small budget, and a limited staff. Despite these handicaps, CITES has managed to control the burgeoning international market for plants and wildlife, and has also helped stem illegal trading in endangered and threatened species. By halting trade in sea turtles, big cats (such as leopards, cheetahs, and tigers) and exotic birds, CITES has prevented the populations of these animals from dropping to critical levels.

Yet, like the ESA, CITES also has its share of controversy. The African elephant is a case in point. Outside of Africa the African elephant is a majestic, sympathetic animal. Westerners were horrified to learn that African elephant

The cheetah is considered critically endangered under the international treaty CITES, and it is protected from trade and hunting.

herds were decimated in the 1970s and 1980s to feed a growing demand for raw ivory. Sometimes called "white gold," ivory's soaring value on the world market (in 1970 it brought $2.50 per pound; by the end of the decade the price was $60 per pound) led to the poaching of thousands of elephants merely for their tusks. According to one estimate, 100,000 adult African elephants were killed each year in Africa from 1978 through 1988. This caused the population of free-roaming African elephants to plummet from 1.2 million in 1978 to 109,000 in 1988.

To Africans, however, elephants are dangerous brutes that trample crops and demolish villages. To African farmers trying to eke out a living from the hard-baked ground, elephants are worse than locusts, for they can instantly destroy what might have taken years to build. As Raymond Bonner writes in *At the Hand of Man: Peril and Hope for African Wildlife:* "A herd of elephants goes through an area like a slow tornado, snapping off branches and uprooting trees, leaving devastation behind."

Some African farmers have been brought to the brink of starvation and economic ruin by elephants. In 1990 a

Elephant herds diminished in the 1970s and 1980s due to the thriving ivory trade. Thousands of elephants were killed and stripped of their tusks to meet the demand for ivory.

woman who farmed five acres in western Laikipia, a district of Kenya, with her husband wrote to a prominent African wildlife official:

> We settled there in 1981, but to date, we have never harvested any maize or potatoes. Our casuarinas [hardwood trees] have never thrived, our bananas have been uprooted by the same jumbos you are protecting. . . . Come June/July/and August, the jumbos are there to share what we have toiled for and to uproot what we have planted. . . . Please consider that thousands of wananchi [people] are suffering because of these same jumbos you are protecting.

From this perspective, it is little wonder, as African conservationist David Western notes, that "Hungry African farmers . . . would gladly see all elephants eradicated."

In October 1989 the clash of opposing views of the elephant came to a head at a CITES meeting in Switzerland. Some countries, such as the United States, pushed hard to make the elephant an endangered rather than threatened species, and to totally ban ivory trading.

But many African nations and some conservationists disagreed. These countries desperately needed the money they received from legal ivory sales; moreover, as David Western argues, a ban "would exaggerate the problems with wildlife in Africa because African nations use the revenue from ivory to help finance their conservation programs."

In addition, a total ban ignored the fact that only East African countries were losing elephants. Elephant herds in Botswana, Zimbabwe, and South Africa were growing, not diminishing. These southern countries argued that they should not be punished for problems elsewhere and that their economies and their citizens would suffer without the ability to reasonably limit their elephant populations by killing selected animals (a process known as culling) and then selling the ivory.

The arguments of the southern Africans lost. After raucous debate, CITES moved the elephant from Appendix II to Appendix I (formally assigning it endangered status) and voted to ban ivory trading as of January 18, 1990. Critics of the ban charged that the industrialized nations were

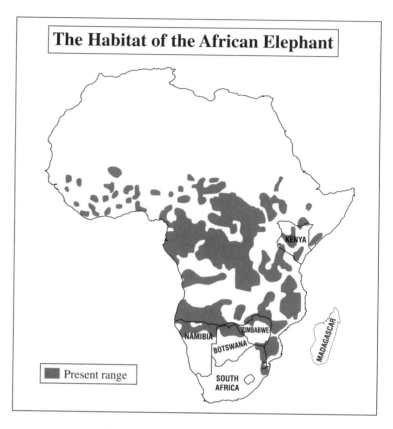

The Habitat of the African Elephant

KENYA

ZIMBABWE

NAMIBIA

BOTSWANA

MADAGASCAR

SOUTH AFRICA

Present range

forcing their will onto a situation they did not understand, and that Western sympathies were misplaced. "At one stroke of the pen consciences were appeased," wrote Richard C. Morais in *Forbes* magazine. "The West had done its part in saving the elephant."

Once the ban took effect, the price of ivory dropped sharply, and elephant herds began to increase. Unfortunately, African citizens continued to suffer from elephant rampages. Since an average elephant requires about three hundred pounds of food per day (mainly bark and grasses), the growing numbers of elephants wreaked havoc on vegetation and crops. Now the African nations had the worst of both worlds: more elephants, and more damage, without the much-needed capital culling the herd could bring.

The African nations of Zimbabwe, Botswana, and Namibia began pressing for approval to make a one-time sale of fifty-nine tons of stockpiled ivory to Japan in 1999, based on evidence that their combined elephant herd of approximately 150,000 was growing. Industrialized nations such as the United States and France opposed relaxing the ban because they feared that mass killing of elephants throughout the continent would begin again.

A compromise

Finally, in June 1997, a compromise was reached at the CITES meeting in Harare, Zimbabwe. Botswana, Namibia, and Zimbabwe were granted permission to sell fifty-nine tons of ivory from culled elephants to Japan in 1999. However, before this sale can occur, the three nations have to install, and CITES has to approve, a reporting and monitoring system that will prevent excessive killing and poaching.

As the reactions to the agreement indicated, a wide gulf existed between the two sides:

"This [compromise] is a triumph for sanity, objectivity and for recognizing developing countries' ability to make their own decisions on natural resource management," said Dick Pitman of the Zambezi Society of Zimbabwe.

"We are extremely disappointed and fearful for the future of the elephant throughout Africa," said Wayne Parcelle of the Humane Society of the United States.

Holes in the safety net

In some respects, laws and treaties such as the ESA and CITES are like huge safety nets that prevent endangered species from extinction. However, "holes" in these nets sometimes let endangered species fall through.

In some circumstances, for example, a special provision of CITES allows a member nation to take a reservation on a certain species. This means that the

These ornate ivory products were confiscated under laws banning ivory trade. Several African nations have recently received permission to begin selling ivory from culled elephants.

country does not have to abide by any of the restrictions placed on that species by CITES. Since the CITES secretariat, which administers the treaty, has no enforcement powers, the effectiveness of CITES depends on each nation's willingness to support it.

While the ESA does contain enforcement powers, ways have been found to punch "holes" through this net as well. One notable example occurred in the battle over the Tellico Dam.

In the late 1960s the Tennessee Valley Authority (TVA) began building the Tellico Dam on the Little Tennessee River. Although primarily built to generate electricity, when finished the dam would also create a lake by flooding a valley.

In 1973, before Tellico was finished, biologist David Etnier discovered a tiny, three-inch-long fish in the Little Tennessee River whose existence was previously unknown. He called it a snail darter. Since the fish apparently lived only in a section of the river that was to be flooded by the dam, the completion of the dam would destroy the darter's habitat.

Environmental groups successfully petitioned to have the snail darter declared an endangered species; under the terms of the recently enacted ESA, since the completion of Tellico would take the snail darter by wiping out its habitat, work on the dam stopped.

Arguments over preservation of the snail darter's habitat blocked construction of the Tellico Dam in Tennessee for six years. The dam was eventually built and the snail darter was later discovered in other bodies of water.

Supporters of the dam filed suit to resume construction, taking their case all the way to the U.S. Supreme Court. In 1978 the Court ruled in favor of the snail darter by a vote of 6-3. A tiny fish had halted a massive construction project in its tracks.

However, many members of Congress supported the dam and introduced a bill that would exempt Tellico from the ESA. In speaking out in support of this bill, Tennessee senator Howard Baker called the snail darter "that awful beast . . . the bane of my existence, the nemesis of my golden years, the bold perverter of the Endangered Species Act." Although he spoke somewhat in jest, Baker was expressing the frustrated realization of many members in Congress that the ESA could give a three-inch fish the power to block a multimillion-dollar dam.

The bill passed, and Tellico was completed in 1979. The dam's completion did indeed flood the valley, which, presumably, destroyed the habitat of the snail darter. However, one year later the snail darter was found living in several other bodies of water.

Although the snail darter appeared to qualify for ESA protection, in the end a way was found to circumvent the law.

Other strategies

Other safety nets for endangered species have also been flawed. A "total" ban on whaling, for example, has turned out to be much less than total.

Having been aggressively hunted for generations, several species of whales were on the verge of extinction by the 1960s, including the blue whale and the bowhead whale. In response, the International Whaling Commission (IWC) set annual quotas of various whale species that could be killed. Some countries, such as the United States and the United Kingdom, halted commercial whaling; others did not. The IWC is a voluntary association of twenty-four whaling nations that regulate and control the hunting of whales, though it has no power to punish violators.

The quota system did little to help the whales. By 1986 the number of bowhead whales had shrunk to an estimated

Opponents of the whaling exemptions claim that whale watching, a thriving business on the west coast of North America, will suffer as hunted whales become aggressive.

4,417. In that year, the IWC imposed a total ban on all commercial whaling.

Again, countries with large whaling industries, primarily Japan, Norway, Russia, and Iceland, disagreed with this decision and continued commercial whaling in defiance of the ban, although on a more limited basis. It is estimated that eleven thousand whales were killed from 1986 to 1995, during the "total" ban on whaling.

The countries that continue whaling argue that they should be allowed to harvest a limited number of animals for food, scientific research, and other purposes. They support their requests with claims that certain species of whales are more abundant than is commonly believed. For example, Norway, which defends the practice of hunting minke whales (a small whale that reaches lengths of about ten meters), claims that approximately 1 million minke whales exist; others say that the number is closer to ten thousand.

October 1997 brought more exemptions to the whaling "ban." Under pressure from the United States, the IWC granted the Makah tribe of Washington State permission to hunt four gray whales per year from 1998 through 2002.

An 1855 treaty with the U.S. government had given the Makah the right to hunt gray whales, but the tribe had ceased whaling in 1926 because the number of animals had dropped sharply. In 1995, with the population up, the Makahs asked to be allowed to go whaling once again.

The death of 4 whales per year may not seem like a lot, but conservationists worried that this exemption would further weaken the ban. Already, to gain Russian support for the Makah exemption, the United States had to agree to let natives of Russia's Chukotka region harvest 120 whales per year.

"This will now open the door for more quota increases," said Representative Jack Metcalf of Washington, who filed a lawsuit against the Makah proposal. "Japan has already stated the desire to allow four villages on the Taiji Peninsula with no subsistence need to be granted a quota. Iceland, Ireland, Norway, China . . . where will it end?"

Whale watching

Others were concerned that the exemptions would mean the end of the lucrative gray whale–watching business on the West Coast. The highly intelligent whales were once known as "devil fish" because they attacked the boats of whalers. In recent years, no longer fearful whales often playfully approach the whale-watching ships. But captains fear that the animals' legendary aggressiveness would return once they realized they were again being hunted, putting boats and passengers in danger.

"[The Makah exemption] might mean the end of the gray whale–watching business on the Pacific Coast," said Jamie Bray, owner of Jamie's Whaling Station in British Columbia. Bray estimated that whale watching in his region generates between $8 and $10 million annually.

Although laws and treaties might seem to give endangered species ironclad protection, subsequent events have often proven otherwise. In reality, no species is ever truly "safe"; too many factors can intervene to place a species at risk, even when it seems protection is guaranteed.

2

The Causes of Extinction

As LONG AS there has been life on earth, there has been extinction. In fact, natural selection predicts that extinction is the ultimate fate of every species that has ever existed on this planet. Although today as many as 40 to 50 million species exist in the world, between 5 and 50 *billion* species have existed during the course of life on earth. This means that the millions of species alive today represent less than 1 percent of the total number of all species. The average life of a plant or animal species is "only" 4 million years.

Nature and extinction

Earth history is conventionally described by a geologic time scale divided into periods of millions of years. Modern scientists believe major mass extinctions occurred at the end of the Ordovician, Devonian, Permian, Triassic, and Cretaceous periods.

The most well known extinction occurred at the end of the Cretaceous period, 65 million years ago, when the mighty dinosaurs vanished, leaving behind their bones and a mystery that intrigues people to this day. The reason why these great creatures vanished from the planet they ruled for so long remains unknown.

Yet the dinosaurs were not the only creatures to be wiped out. It is estimated that 70 percent of all known species became extinct during this time; whatever caused this cataclysmic event in the earth's history spared few species from its devastating effects. Yet some of those that survived, including crocodiles, sharks, frogs, salamanders, turtles, and even mammals, continue to exist in modern times.

The shark is an example of a successful species that is largely the same today as it was millions of years ago; scientists would say it is very well adapted in terms of evolution. All species must adapt to environmental change and competition with other species to continue to exist; those that don't become extinct.

Although evolution is usually measured in many thousands of years, sometimes it can occur quite rapidly. One example is the peppered moth, a species found in England. A majority of this species was originally light gray, with a few dark-colored exceptions. Because the light gray moths' coloring acted as camouflage, blending in with light-colored tree trunks and allowing the moths to go undetected by birds, light gray moths survived to reproduce in greater numbers. But when soot from coal-burning factories began blackening the trees, the light-colored moths stood out like whipped cream on chocolate and became easy marks for birds. Now the dark moths more often survived long enough to reproduce: Within fifty years, the dark moths predominated.

Other natural events can also lead to species extinction. A volcanic eruption, a sudden rise or fall in sea level,

As tree trunks in England blackened from soot, the peppered moth's coloring darkened to adapt to its changing environment. Such adaptation is necessary for a species' survival.

disease, a change in climate, and the introduction or emergence of a predator are some factors that can threaten a species' ability to survive. Yet the consequences of extinction are not necessarily always bad. If some carnivorous dinosaurs had escaped extinction, it is conceivable that mammals—including humans—might not have become the dominant species in the world today.

On occasion, extinction may even be beneficial. Mark Sagoff, a philosopher at the University of Maryland, noting that the AIDS virus apparently originated in a species of monkey in Africa, asks: "Who could deny that the world would have been spared great agony had that species, a century ago, gone extinct?"

Enter humanity

Today, some scientists fear that another period of mass extinction is imminent, primarily caused not by natural phenomena but by human activities. Pollution, hunting, habitat destruction and development, and population pressures may be setting the stage for yet another wave of death to engulf the earth.

"Ecologists say that the greatest difference between the present mass extinction and those of the past . . . is that today's extinctions are entirely due to the activities of a single species—*Homo sapiens,* or human beings," says Norman Myers, a leading conservation expert. "We are the sole species in the history of life to have the capacity to cause a mass extinction of many other species."

People have had an enormous impact on other species. Fossil records indicate that the arrival of people in a particular region has meant the departure of species. People first appeared in Hawaii approximately two thousand years ago. Since that time, over 100 species of birds and 273 species of plants have become extinct. Ornithologists (scientists who study birds) have estimated that as many as 2,000 species of birds have vanished since the Pacific Islands were settled.

Of course, birds are not the only animal species adversely affected by the presence of people. Madagascar, a tropical island 220 miles off the southeastern African coast, was once home to approximately forty different kinds of lemurs, a relative of monkeys and apes. However, about two thousand years ago, the first people on Mada-gascar began killing the lemurs for food. They also cut down the trees in which lemurs lived to clear land for homes and farms. Today at least twenty types of lemurs have vanished from the island.

Plants have also been adversely affected by humanity. The southern tip of Africa supports a diverse population of eighty-five hundred plant species. Within the last century, thirty-six species have become extinct and another six hundred are at risk, primarily because people have brought in plants from other countries that compete with the native plants for space and sunlight. In South Africa, for example, the Wildlife and Environmental Society of Southern Africa offers information on locating the "28 alien plant invaders in Natal" (Kwazulu Natal is one of the smallest provinces of South Africa) and what to do when one of these "invaders" is discovered.

Hunting and habitat destruction have reduced the types of lemurs on Madagascar by about one-half.

Water pollution has also affected species. Over the past one hundred years, the construction of dams and canals, as well as pollution, has caused the extinction of twenty-one species of freshwater mussels and clams in the Mississippi and St. Lawrence river basins of North America.

Development in the United States

Humanity's profound impact on other species is sometimes unavoidable. Clearing land to build homes, businesses, and towns; converting forests into crop-producing farmland; and paving over fields to build roads, hospitals, and schools is intended not to harm other species but to provide basic human necessities.

For example, when the Pilgrims landed at Plymouth, Massachusetts, in 1620, they faced an immense forest. This great eastern forest stretched almost without interruption from Maine to Florida and from Massachusetts to Missouri—approximately 600 million acres.

To the Pilgrims, who were used to the towns and villages of England, the forests were terrifying. William Bradford, one of the leaders of the Plymouth Colony, called America a "hideous and desolate wilderness." In the interest of their own survival, the Pilgrims began cutting down trees to build homes, farms, and towns.

During the 1870s, a greater proportion of the great eastern forest disappeared than the world's tropical rain forests lost in the 1980s.

The effects of this massive change to the landscape must have been catastrophic to untold numbers of species. Although no one knows for certain, it is likely that many life forms became extinct as the wilderness gave way to civilization. Yet it is also likely that the United States of America would not have been able to grow, prosper, and become one of the leading countries of the world without this type of development.

Developing the rain forests in Third World countries

Today this situation is repeating itself in some Third World countries. As they try to strengthen their national economies, and raise their citizens' standard of living, some nations are developing rain forests and other natural areas that are home to thousands, perhaps millions, of plant and animal species.

Although these countries are aware of the danger that development poses to species, often their major resource is land, a resource that is useless unless it is developed. Official policy may be to protect species and conserve their habitat, but in practice the needs of their people come first.

The situation in Brazil is typical. Although Brazil is a large country, not enough land is cleared for people to live on. Since much of the developed land is owned by wealthy landowners, the poor naturally turn to the rain forest, where land is plentiful and available.

The Brazilian government encourages people to move into the rain forest both to relieve overcrowding in the rest of the country and to develop the region and harvest its resources. To speed the process along, the government has built roads such as the 3,350-mile Trans-Amazon Highway (longer than the distance between New York and San Francisco) directly through the Amazon jungles.

The effects of this type of activity on the species that live in the rain forest are the subject of intense study. It is

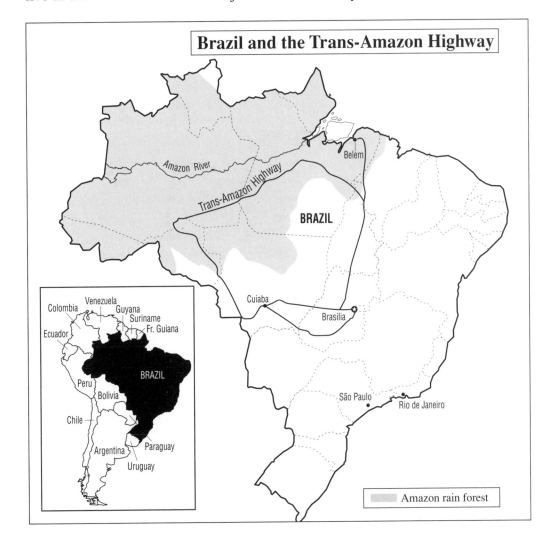

Brazil and the Trans-Amazon Highway

estimated that tropical rain forests contain two-thirds or more of the world's species of plants or animals. Since it is believed that there could be up to 40 million undiscovered species on earth, it is probable that many of these are in the rain forest, and might become extinct before being discovered.

Today, the rain forests are under increasing pressure from humanity. Everywhere, the rain forests are disappearing; since 1960, the tropical rain forests of Africa have been reduced by as much as 75 percent. In January 1998, Brazil announced that the extent of the destruction of the Amazon rain forest nearly tripled between 1990 and 1995. Those that want to save the rain forests say it's foolish to develop such areas blindly, arguing that some of the species that are being unwittingly destroyed might ultimately prove beneficial to humanity. They point out that currently, about one-fourth of all prescription drugs come from rain forest plants.

Yet simply preserving land for the sake of species survival, while noble, often does little to help a Third World country or its people. In fact, it may even hurt; when 170 square miles of forest in southern Madagascar was designated as Ranamafano National Park in 1991, over seventy thousand people who had brought their cattle into that area or cut wood for much-needed income were suddenly forbidden from doing either. This action displaced these people from earning a living.

Pollution

An unfortunate consequence of development has been pollution. It is estimated that approximately 15 million tons of soot and dust are suspended in the earth's atmosphere from human activity. Pollution has seeped into virtually every ecological system on earth; even the middle of the vast Pacific Ocean, once thought to be one of the cleanest areas on earth, has been polluted.

Obviously, as pollution has worked its way into the land, water, and air, it has adversely affected many species.

The bald eagle is a typical example of how pollution harms a species. As the symbol of the United States, the

© Wicks/Rothco. Used with permission.

bald eagle occupies a special place in the hearts and minds of most Americans; the bird's stern expression and regal bearing seem to embody American patriotism. Thus it came as a shock when it was revealed in the 1960s that the bald eagle was dying out, possibly headed for extinction.

The problem for the bald eagle was the pesticide DDT (dichloro-diphenyl-trichloroethane). Widely sprayed on crops and over ponds and marshes to kill insects, the toxic chemical compound was contaminating fish and other vertebrates that the bald eagle eats. Once inside the bird's body, DDT was causing the eggs of female eagles to become thin and brittle from insufficient calcium. Many of these eggs were unable to be incubated and failed to hatch.

A plummeting reproduction rate combined with loss of habitat and overhunting caused the number of bald eagles to sharply decline. While as many as 250,000 eagles lived in North America before the industrial revolution, by the mid-1960s fewer than 500 nesting pairs were left in the United States. The bird was placed on the endangered species list, and extinction seemed very possible.

Fortunately, the bald eagle has rebounded. Banning toxins such as DDT, preserving habitat, and preventing hunting resulted in a rise in the eagle population to approximately four thousand pairs of nesting adults in the lower forty-eight states by 1994. That year, the FWS upgraded the bird's status from endangered to threatened in all but three of those states. (Alaska has a healthy population of bald eagles.)

For every good-news story like the recovery of the bald eagle, however, dozens of others prove that pollution has put species at risk. Factories belching smoke and other pollutants into the air, toxic substances leaching out of landfills and contaminating soil and groundwater, toxic wastes dumped into rivers and oceans, carbon monoxide and other gases from internal combustion engines, acid rain produced by the combustion of fossil fuels . . . all of these and more are contributing to an immense assault on species around the globe.

No region on earth is safe from the effects of pollution. Norwegian researchers have warned that the survival rate of first-year polar bear cubs has dropped from 75 percent to 50 percent over the last decade. One possible reason is that the bears have extremely high concentrations of PCBs, compounds with various industrial applications that are extremely toxic environmental contaminants, in their fat. This pollutant has found its way into lactating females' milk, and is being passed on to the newborn cubs.

A ban on DDT, a chemical compound that caused bald eagles' egg shells to break easily, has allowed more young bald eagles to survive.

The *Exxon Valdez* oil spill

Despite progress made in cleaning up the environment, pollution remains a serious threat to species. On March 24, 1989, for example, the oil tanker *Exxon Valdez* ran aground on Bligh Reef in Prince William Sound, Alaska. Almost 11 million gallons of crude oil gushed from the stricken tanker, making it the largest oil spill in U.S. history.

Despite the best efforts of cleanup crews, the oil moved along the Alaskan coastline throughout the spring, fouling a national forest, four national wildlife refuges, three national parks, five state parks, four state critical habitat areas, and a state game sanctuary. (Oil eventually reached shorelines nearly six hundred miles southwest of Bligh Reef.)

The oil wreaked havoc among species. According to findings published in 1996 by the American Fisheries Society, among the animals lost were 300 harbor seals, 2,800 sea otters, 250,000 birds, and (possibly) 13 killer whales. Although the spill did not affect any endangered species in this case, a similar spill in an area where such species did exist could completely destroy or seriously harm it.

Effects of the oil spill continue to ricochet through Alaska's wildlife community. In 1993 the Pacific herring population plummeted due to a viral disease and a fungus possibly caused by the oil, resulting in a moratorium on commercial fishing of herring for four years. Besides possibly losing thirteen members, a pod of thirty-six killer whales produced no young in the two years following the spill. By 1996 the pod had not yet recovered; it was losing more members than were being born, and the whales' complex social structure appeared to be deteriorating.

Pollution, development, and other human activities have all contributed to an overall decline of species around the world.

3

Hunting

ON JUNE 3, 1844, the last great auk was killed in Iceland. A large, flightless bird with a black grooved bill, the great auk had once been plentiful along both coasts of the North Atlantic, particularly in Newfoundland, Nova Scotia, and New Brunswick. The birds nested on low ledges in rocky coastal areas, which is why they were vulnerable to attack by predators, including humans.

Unable to escape by flying, the birds were easy prey for early explorers and mariners, who killed thousands at a time for food. The bird was also hunted for its feathers, which were used as stuffing for pillows and beds, and for its carcass, which could be rendered for cooking oil.

Because the female great auk laid only one egg at a time, the bird's population plummeted due to overhunting. Finally the great auk vanished from the earth.

Hunting has adversely impacted many species. Excessive hunting has destroyed some species and driven others to the brink of extinction. Even today, with a greater awareness of the problems many species face, and numerous laws and safeguards, hunting remains a serious threat to many creatures.

Vanished

The great auk was not the only species to be hunted into extinction. At one time the passenger pigeon was the most abundant bird on earth; some ornithologists calculate that one out of every four birds in North America was a passenger pigeon before the New World was explored. The bird flew in great flocks that stretched for miles, filling the sky like a giant thundercloud. "The light of noon-day was obscured as by an eclipse," wrote naturalist and painter John James Audubon upon watching one massive flock of pigeons pass overhead. Hunters killed the birds by the millions, for food and for sport. Because they seemed so plentiful, no one paid attention to the bird's diminishing numbers until it was too late. Belatedly, an effort was made to save the species, but to no avail. On September 1, 1914, the last passenger pigeon (named Martha) died in captivity in the Cincinnati Zoo.

The ivory-billed woodpecker is another bird that excess hunting helped to wipe out. The largest North American woodpecker, measuring approximately twenty inches (about the size of a crow), the ivory-billed woodpecker was once plentiful over much of the southeastern United States, ranging as far west as Texas and Oklahoma. The bird's main source of food was the larvae of wood-boring insects found in dying trees. As the forests were developed, the woodpecker's habitat steadily contracted.

Yet hunting also played a major role in the bird's demise. Considered a delicacy, many thousands were killed for food. "People consider them better than ducks," wrote one observer in 1893.

Between hunting and loss of habitat, the ivory-billed woodpecker population was in extreme distress by the mid-1940s. Forty years later, an ornithologist searching through the remaining bogs and forests of the southeastern United States could not find any of the birds. Although a few people reported seeing ivory-billed woodpeckers in a forest in Cuba, it is now feared that that population is also gone, and that the bird has become extinct.

Sometimes, even if people belatedly realize that a species has been hunted to

The great auk, a victim of overhunting, has been extinct for over 150 years.

Passenger pigeons, once plentiful in North America, were hunted into extinction. The last passenger pigeon died in 1914.

near-extinction and try to preserve it, these efforts are not enough to keep it from disappearing.

For example, the heath hen, a subspecies of the prairie chicken, was abundant from Maine to Virginia at the time the Massachusetts Bay colonists first arrived on the shores of North America. A medium-sized grouse, the heath hen's preferred habitat was the grasslands within a forest. The colonists also preferred this type of area because transforming it into farmland did not involve cutting down and removing trees.

Once people found the heath hen, they also discovered that it tasted good. Easy to catch, the heath hen was soon a staple of the colonists' diet.

Relentless hunting, coupled with habitat loss, quickly reduced the heath hen population. At the time of the American Revolution, the numbers of heath hens had noticeably declined. By 1840, the heath hen had disappeared from many of the regions where it had once been plentiful and was found only in Long Island, Pennsylvania, New Jersey, and a few other places.

By 1870, the only known heath hen population left existed on Martha's Vineyard, an island off the Massachusetts coast. Finally, realizing that the fowl was headed for extinction, people took action; in 1908, a sixteen-hundred-acre refuge was established to protect the birds. At that time, just fifty heath hens were left.

Initially, the heath hen thrived in its new home, where hunting was forbidden. The population soared to two thousand by 1915, and it seemed as if people had managed to save the bird from extinction, but nature had other plans. In 1916, a fire destroyed much of the bird's breeding area. The following winter was unusually harsh and brought a large influx of predatory goshawks. The fire, the weather, and the goshawks caused the heath hen population to plummet once more, and a poultry disease brought to Martha's Vineyard by wild turkeys killed many of the remaining birds.

By 1927, just thirteen heath hens were alive. One year later, a single bird was all that remained of a species that had once numbered in the thousands. After existing by itself for several years, this lone survivor was last seen on March 11, 1932. Natural forces had finished what hunting had begun.

Extinction has also been the fate of numerous other North American species. Between 1885 and 1962, over a billion pounds of blue pike were pulled from the waters of Lake Erie. Today the blue pike has ceased to exist. The silver trout, native to just two lakes in western New Hampshire, has also disappeared. Gone too is the badlands bighorn, a relative of the Rocky Mountain bighorn sheep once found in great numbers throughout the upper Great Plains.

Modern and prehistoric extinction

Species have been hunted to extinction throughout the world. In New Zealand the moa, a unique flightless bird similar to an ostrich, was hunted into oblivion for its tasty flesh.

In Africa by 1860, European settlers had wiped out two species that were once plentiful: the blaubok, a relative of the antelope, and the quagga, which resembled a pony.

For sheer speed of extinction, however, it is doubtful that anything can equal the demise of Steller's sea cow. In

Some researchers believe that mastodons and other ice-age mammals were hunted into oblivion by prehistoric people.

1741, Russian sailors first found this relative of the manatee in the waters of the Bering Sea near the Komandorskiye Islands. When the sailors realized that the large mammal was edible, the killing began; word spread to other ships, and by 1768—a mere twenty-seven years after it was discovered—Steller's sea cow was gone.

Humanity has proven itself so adept at hunting that some scientists believe that humans were responsible for a mass extinction of numerous large animals in North America that occurred at the end of the last ice age (approximately ten thousand years ago). Creatures such as woolly mammoths, mastodons, saber-toothed tigers, giant ground sloths, and others are now believed to have been wiped out by prehistoric hunters.

Today many species are legally protected from hunting. Yet this has not necessarily meant that they are safe.

Cultural differences

Rhinoceroses have walked the earth for about 50 million years. At one time there were more than thirty different types of rhinos. Today, however, just five rhino species are left: the Sumatran, Javan, Indian, white, and black rhinos. According to the International Rhino Foundation, only 13,500 rhinos are left in the entire world, and all five species are tottering on the verge of extinction.

Because the rhino population is in such peril, hunting them is strictly prohibited. Yet rhinos are hunted for their horns despite the ban. In many African and Asian countries, powdered rhino horn is the central ingredient in folk medicines, including those used to increase sexual performance. In some Middle Eastern countries, primarily Yemen, rhino horns are used to make the handles of special ornamental daggers called *djambias*.

A poacher can earn thousands of dollars for a single rhino horn. This is an enormous temptation for residents of poor nations, who struggle to feed their families. In one night they can make more money than they can from an entire year of farming.

In Zimbabwe, poachers reduced a population of one hundred white rhinos to less than five in eighteen months. In desperation, game officials have resorted to dehorning some rhinos (which can be done without hurting the animal) to make them an unattractive target for poachers. A ban on all commercial trading of rhinoceros products instituted by CITES in 1977 has had little effect.

A rhino in Namibia is dehorned. Since rhinos are killed for their highly prized horns, game officials hope that removing the horns will discourage poaching.

As prices for rhino horn climb ever higher, the risk for the animals becomes even greater. As long as some cultures value their horns, rhinos will continue to be threatened. There are many reasons why some cultures value the continued hunting of endangered species. In Africa, killing an elephant has special significance for the Masai, for example. The Masai spear elephants to demonstrate their bravery. Other African groups use the tough hide of a rhino to make shields strong enough to deflect spears. A tradition of the Boran tribe is for the man to carry a whip made from a rhino's tail when his wife gives birth to a son. Another Boran custom is for men who show great bravery in killing an animal to wear bracelets carved from elephant tusks.

These traditional uses for endangered species continue to put them in jeopardy. It also makes it hard to formulate a policy on preserving the species that is fair to all sides.

Black market trade

It is estimated that between $10 and $20 billion in plants and wild animals are illegally traded around the world each year. Much of this black market trade involves endangered plants and animals—another reason that endangered species are still hunted today.

Endangered species are bought for many reasons: as pets, as collector's items, as ingredients in folk medicines

Rhino populations are severely depleted due to the high demand for rhino horn, which is used to make folk medicines and ceremonial daggers. For many poachers, the possibility of earning a high income offsets the risk of being caught.

(tiger bone, like rhino horn, is a common, prized ingredient in Asian folk medicines), and even as food. All of these give poachers an incentive to hunt these species, and drive the populations closer to extinction.

"You go into these jungles where there once were abundant birds and parrots, and now they're empty," maintains biologist George Schaller, describing the rain forests of South America in the *New York Times Magazine:*

> Collectors removed immature birds before they had time to breed. Demand from the pet trade stripped those jungles like a disease. Who knows how many ways the loss of the birds will upset the balance of life in those jungles? But it will.

Endangered species are primarily hunted and sold in Third World countries, because their undeveloped land supplies habitat for many exotic animals.

As for motivation, people hunt, capture, and sell endangered species mainly to earn money. In Peru, a sloth can be sold for $400, which is more than three times the monthly minimum wage.

Endangered species for sale

In Madagascar, home to many unique species, a burgeoning population has placed severe economic pressure on its citizens. The island's population jumped from 6 million in 1960 to 12 million in 1997, and is expected to double again by 2015. To feed all these people, jungles are being converted to rice paddies and grazeland. This destroys the habitat for many endangered species, making it easy for hunters to catch and sell them on the black market. Madagascar has become one of the premier sources for black market smuggling of endangered species.

In an article in the *New York Times Magazine* about trade in endangered animals, a man from Madagascar defended his hunting of rare radiated tortoises, which have brilliantly colored shells: "I have to eat. I have to feed myself and my family, and the fishing has been nearly used up. We are human. We have to eat."

To him, environmentalists and others who want to put him in jail for catching tortoises have their priorities

Radiated tortoises on Madagascar are endangered and killing them is illegal. However, people who are forced to hunt the tortoises to sustain their families complain that environmentalists care more about animals than people.

confused: "They have the problem backward—let the tortoise live, so I can starve."

While the price that this man and his partners get for a boatload of illegally captured tortoises is only about 30 cents each, the price that people in other countries will pay for such creatures is staggering. Such rare animals as a komodo dragon from Indonesia, a woolly spider monkey from Brazil, and an orangutan from Sumatra can command up to $50,000. Other valuable species include a hyacinth macaw from South America ($20,000), an oenpelli python from Australia ($30,000), a black palm cockatoo from Indonesia ($20,000), and a plowshare tortoise from Madagascar ($20,000).

With a growing demand for exotic and endangered species around the world, the black market trade will continue. And as long as people in Third World countries have difficulty providing for themselves and their families, it is going to be hard to convince them not to hunt endangered species.

4

The Race Against Extinction

Today, Species extinction has become an ethical issue around which thousands of people around the world have rallied. But as people demand more and more from the earth, species are forced into steadily shrinking corners of the globe.

For centuries, a species was only protected when it provided an important food source for people. This was the reason that colonial Newport, Rhode Island, passed a law in 1639 restricting deer hunting, to allow more individuals to reproduce. The idea of saving all species, in order to shield them from extinction, was not considered.

A history of extermination

Usually, it was extermination, not salvation, that people had in mind for a particular species. The wolf, for example, was deliberately hunted to near-extinction in North America. Because wolves had a reputation as fearsome, vicious killers that would attack without mercy or warning, humans waged war on wolves for centuries. Governmental policy often encouraged this wanton destruction. In 1630 the Massachusetts Bay Colony offered one penny for every wolf shot. Through 1970 the Canadian province of Ontario paid $69,996 for the heads of 1,255 eastern timber wolves, 2,047 coyotes, and 43 coyote and wolf pups.

In fact, wolves were so hated that in 1905 Montana passed a law requiring veterinarians to infect captured wolves with a mite that caused mange, a debilitating condition characterized by hair loss and skin infections. The infected wolves were then set free to contaminate other packs.

Usually, however, no formal policy toward a hunted species existed. This attitude began to change in the 1880s, when it suddenly became clear that the American bison was on the verge of extinction.

The largest land animal in North America, the bison, also called the buffalo, once roamed the entire continent in herds that numbered in the hundreds of thousands. Although usually associated with the American West, the bison once ranged as far east as Washington, D.C.

Even after hunters wiped out the buffalo in the eastern United States, an estimated 60 million bison still lived west of the Mississippi in 1830. Before long, however, these animals too were being slaughtered. Alarmed at the ceaseless killing, in 1843 the famous naturalist and bird

An 1874 newspaper illustration shows a hunter holding up the hide of a buffalo. The great demand for buffalo hides in the nineteenth century contributed to the demise of the animal.

Buffalo are slaughtered on the Kansas Pacific Railroad. The buffalo were killed along the railroads to feed the construction crew and, after the railroads' completion, for the enjoyment of the passengers.

artist John James Audubon said: "Like the Great Auk, before many years the Buffalo will vanish. Surely this should not be permitted?"

The carnage peaked with the coming of the railroad to the western United States. The workers who built the railroad needed food, and the bison provided an easily available source; hunters killed enormous numbers of animals to feed the construction crews. One hunter, William F. Cody, killed over four thousand bison in twelve months, earning the nickname "Buffalo Bill."

The railroad cut the Great Plains in half, splitting the bison population into southern and northern herds. Greatly in demand for their hides, which were made into leather goods, and for their tongues, considered a dining delicacy, bison were killed at an appalling rate, beginning with the southern herd in the early 1870s. Between 1873 and 1874, sales of 100,000 bison hides were recorded each *day* in Fort Worth, Texas, alone. No animal population could long withstand depletion that drastic.

Even worse was the wanton killing of bison merely for amusement. In 1869, Theodore R. Davis wrote in *Harper's Magazine:*

> It would seem to be hardly possible to imagine a more novel sight than a small band of buffalo loping along within a few hundred feet of a railroad train in rapid motion, while the

passengers are engaged in shooting, from every available window, with rifles, carbines, and revolvers. An American scene, certainly.

By the last decade of the nineteenth century, this "American scene" had succeeded in virtually destroying the bison. William T. Hornaday, chief taxidermist for the National Museum in Washington, D.C., estimated that only 541 bison remained in America, and a little over a thousand existed on the entire North American continent. It had taken less than a human lifetime to kill 60 million animals.

Conservation

This revelation stunned many people, especially Hornaday. In his youth he had hunted and killed animals all over the world, sending his catch to museums to be mounted and exhibited. But the realization that the once mighty bison herds had been reduced to a pitiful handful of animals galvanized him to a different type of action. He launched a public campaign to save the bison.

The bison was the first step on what became a lifelong road of species preservation for Hornaday. The former hunter became an ardent conservationist. A relentless crusader against extinction, Hornaday founded the Permanent Wild Life Protection Fund, the first organization in the United States dedicated to stopping the destruction of species.

Hornaday wrote frankly about changing deeply ingrained attitudes toward killing animals. In 1913 he wrote:

> Today, the thing that stares me in the face every waking hour, like a grisly spectre with bloody fang and claw, is the extermination of species. To me, this is a horrible thing. It is wholesale murder, no less. It is a capital crime, and a black disgrace to the races of civilized mankind.

At the same time that Hornaday was campaigning against extinction, John Muir, a Scottish immigrant to the United States, was also becoming interested in conserving nature. Muir suffered a blinding eye injury as a young man in 1867, while working in a carriage parts shop in Indianapolis. When he recovered, he resolved to use his sight to view natural beauty rather than human-made creations.

Muir began traveling around the world. His passionate writing about nature's beauty quickly gained a large following, and by 1890, Muir was a famous conservationist. In that year, Congress created three national parks—Yosemite, Sequoia, and Kings Canyon (originally called General Grant)—thanks in large part to Muir's influence. In 1903, Muir spent several days with U.S. president Theodore Roosevelt at Yosemite National Park, talking about the threats to forests and other natural resources and the need for conservation.

Roosevelt and Muir were of like minds. The president was already an ardent conservationist; in 1887, he and some friends had founded the Boone and Crockett Club, which had as one of its objectives "the preservation of the large game of the country."

Roosevelt knew the importance of species preservation. "Wild beasts and birds are by right not the property merely of people today," he said, "but the property of the unborn generations, whose belongings we have no right to squander."

President Theodore Roosevelt (left) and John Muir on Glacier Point above Yosemite Valley in California. Roosevelt and Muir were driving forces behind the creation and preservation of national parks.

He backed up his words by deeds. During Roosevelt's tenure as president, government land reserves increased from 45 million to 195 million acres, five new national parks were established (Crater Lake, Wind Cave, Platt Park, Sully Hill, and Mesa Verde), and eighteen national monuments were established. In 1903 Roosevelt began the National Wildlife Refuge System (a network of public lands set aside for the conservation of fish, wildlife, and plants) by designating three-acre Pelican Island in Florida as a pelican and heron rookery. Fifty-one wildlife refuges were established during Roosevelt's presidency.

Others rallied to the conservation cause. In Great Britain, Henry Salt wrote the prospecies essay "Animals' Rights Considered in Relation to Social Progress" in 1891.

Twelve years later, the Society for the Preservation of the Wild Fauna of the Empire was founded in England. In America, Audubon Societies popped up in state after state and were instrumental in passing laws protecting egrets and other birds who were slaughtered merely for the use of their feathers as hat decorations.

Governments also began to act. On May 25, 1900, Congress passed the Lacey Act, which made it a federal offense to ship illegally killed wildlife between states. The law also regulated the sale of bird feathers and other animal products and placed controls on the importation of animals into the United States from other countries.

In 1906 Canada passed the Northwest Game Act, which controlled the taking of fur animals. Ten years later, the United States and Great Britain (acting on Canada's behalf) signed the Migratory Bird Treaty, recognizing migratory birds (birds that crossed the borders of the two countries) as an international resource. In 1918 Congress passed the Migratory Bird Treaty Act, which decreed that all migratory birds and their "parts" (eggs, nests, feathers, etc.) were protected. The act formalized a compact between the United States, Canada, Japan, Mexico, and Russia to protect migratory birds.

The whooping crane

In 1945 the plight of endangered species gained widespread attention when the U.S. Fish and Wildlife Service, the Canadian Wildlife Service, and the National Audubon Society launched

Theodore Roosevelt established five national parks, eighteen national monuments, and fifty-one wildlife refuges during his term in office.

a public campaign to save the whooping crane, the tallest bird in North America. For decades the stately white birds with the distinctive cry had been declining in numbers, due to loss of habitat and a low reproduction rate. By 1938 just twenty-nine "whoopers" existed in the world.

The campaign to save the whooping crane riveted public attention. In the late 1940s, an attempt to track the cranes

on their summer migration from Texas to Canada plunged the entire midwestern United States into "whooper mania." Newspapers and radio stations ran stories urging people to report whooper sightings, and an official who was tracking the bird was besieged with phone calls at his hotel from concerned citizens. The gangly, unusual-looking creature with the long, narrow bill had placed endangered species squarely in the public eye.

Despite more than fifty years of conservation effort, whooping cranes continue to produce few eggs and remain an endangered species.

Unfortunately, the whooping crane, provided with the Aransas National Wildlife Refuge in Texas as a winter home and the Wood Buffalo National Park in Canada and the Platte River Trust in Nebraska as other safe havens, is still endangered. Despite massive amounts of time, money, and effort, the population of whoopers stands at less than 250, and the species remains highly endangered, primarily because of the bird's low reproduction rate. Two eggs are laid each breeding season and usually hatch, but one chick is almost always pushed out of the nest or starved. At this rate, it has been difficult to build up a substantial population of whoopers.

The 1960s, with its emphasis on ecology and cleaning up the earth's environment, further reinforced the need to preserve species. Now came the hard part: figuring out how to save endangered species in a rapidly changing world.

Saving endangered species

At first, it might seem simple: just stop hunting bald eagles, whooping cranes, bison, or whatever species was endangered, and the population would increase. For good measure, create a habitat sanctuary where the animal could live without human interference, and the problem would be solved.

Of course, it has not turned out to be that easy. Species preservation has forced humanity to rethink its place in the world and consider a variety of approaches to try to stop extinction.

Some species have responded favorably to a ban on hunting. Gray whales, which are found in the Pacific Ocean off the North American coast, had been reduced by excessive hunting to just a few thousand by the 1920s. In 1937 the International Whaling Commission (which has jurisdiction on whaling all over the world) banned the hunting of gray whales, and Mexico, to which the whale migrates yearly, established breeding sanctuaries for them. The number of gray whales was already rising when it was placed on the U.S. endangered species list in 1973. In June 1994, with its population up to twenty-four thousand, the gray whale was declared recovered and removed from the list.

Other species that have benefited from a hunting ban include the bison, the American alligator, the sea otter, and the wood duck.

In spite of a ban on hunting Attwater's prairie chicken, the species remains critically endangered due to habitat destruction.

The natural territory of the panda is a fraction of what it once was. Today, the remaining pandas live in this relatively tiny habitat or in captivity in zoos (pictured).

Sometimes, however, merely preventing hunting is not enough; other forces counteract the positive effects of a ban. This is what has happened to Attwater's prairie chicken, a brown, medium-size grouse that once roamed the Gulf Coast of the United States a million strong. Over-hunting and loss of habitat (it is estimated that less than 1 percent of the coastal prairie that it favors still remains) decimated the prairie chicken population. Even though it has long been forbidden to kill a prairie chicken, by 1996 just forty-two animals remained, making it one of the world's most critically endangered species.

Habitat loss has also been pushing the giant panda to-ward extinction. Once widespread throughout China, today there are just one thousand pandas left, all confined to the bamboo forests of southwestern China. Like the prairie chicken, the panda has been protected from hunting for years, but loss of habitat has been an even deadlier foe. Ac-cording to the World Wildlife Fund, suitable habitat for the panda has decreased by 50 percent over the past fifteen years, affecting not only the range of the panda but also the availability of its primary food source, bamboo.

Habitat destruction is responsible for endangering species on almost every continent. The cheetah (Asia), the mountain gorilla (Africa), the maned wolf (South America), the paddlefish (North America), the dalmatian pelican (Europe), and the numbat (Australia) are just a few of the many species that are threatened by loss of habitat.

Trying to save a species by preserving its habitat isn't foolproof, either. Sometimes the strategy works, as in the case of Kirtland's warbler, a songbird found in central Michigan. The bird nests only at the base of young jack pines less than eighteen feet high; it depends on periodic wildfires to generate enough heat to burst open jack pine cones and release the seeds so that young trees can grow. However, when people moved into the area, they fought wildfires, disrupting the natural fire cycle and sabotaging the warbler's reproductive cycle.

By the mid-1990s, just one thousand warblers were known to exist. However, by using controlled burning over habitat set aside for the warbler in Michigan's Lower Peninsula, wildlife officials have been able to get the bird's population growing once again.

In other cases, preserving habitat does not help if species cannot be confined in it. Animals don't abide by artificial boundaries set by humans, such as fences; they go where they can find food. Thus it is easy for a species to roam beyond a protected area. Yellowstone National Park, for example, offers an unspoiled and protected habitat for grizzly bears. However, the bears have difficulty finding food from October through May, when much of the park is snow covered. Then they tend to amble onto private lands, where they threaten humans. More than three-quarters of grizzly bears killed by humans meet their death on private lands.

Captive breeding

Captive breeding is another technique used to perpetuate endangered species. In this method, an animal is bred and its offspring are raised in captivity, ideally only until they can be released into the wild.

The peregrine falcon's population was once dangerously low, but captive breeding has boosted its numbers. The newly released falcons nest in cliffs in the wild and even skyscrapers in urban areas.

Some captive breeding programs have been very successful. By 1975 habitat loss and pesticide use had depleted the peregrine falcon population to fewer than fifty pairs, and extinction seemed likely. But a captive breeding program put the brakes on the bird's slide toward oblivion. Today, peregrine falcons have been released not only into the wild but also in major cities, where skyscrapers substitute for cliffs as nesting sites. By 1995 the peregrine falcon population had risen to more than thirteen hundred pairs.

However, few captive breeding programs have worked as well. The time and effort spent increasing a species in captivity is wasted if the animal is released back into the same circumstances that led to its becoming endangered. This is what happened to the European barn owl. Habitat loss throughout Europe was a major reason for the owl's population decline; though at one point amateur breeders were releasing approximately three thousand captive-bred owls each year in an attempt to restore the bird's numbers, many of these were killed in traffic accidents, by lack of food due to development of natural areas, and other factors that decreased habitat.

Other captive-bred species have suffered similar fates. In the 1970s and 1980s, several hundred captive-bred orangutans were released into the jungles of Borneo and Sumatra. No one knows how many survived, but the orangutan population continued to decline. In January 1993, a meeting of the World Conservation Union's Species Survival Commission concluded that these efforts on behalf of the orangutan had "no conservation value" and should cease.

Unfortunately, it is quite possible that many of the orangutans succumbed to poachers. In areas where poaching remains high, captive breeding programs are almost certainly doomed to fail; instead of helping the species survive, captive breeding merely replenishes the supply of animals for the poachers to prey on. In India's Western Ghats forest, widespread poaching of the lion-tailed macaque scuttled plans to release captive-bred macaques back into the wild, even though the species breeds exceptionally well in captivity.

Overall, captive breeding programs have had a spotty track record. A 1989 study in *Science* magazine found that just 38 percent of all attempts to put captive-bred species back into the wild succeeded. In 1993 Ben Beck, associate director for biological programs at the National Zoo in Washington, D.C., stated in an article in *International Wildlife* that out of 146 reintroduction programs with 126 different species (most of them fish), just 16 had succeeded. According to Beck, a reintroduction program is successful if it creates a population of at least 500 self-sustaining animals. On the short list of successes Beck listed the Canadian wood bison; the bean goose, lesser white-fronted goose, and alpine ibex in Europe; the gharial crocodile in India; and the Galapagos iguana and tortoise.

Cost and controversy

For such a slight success rate, the cost has been enormously high. By 1993 a seven-year program to return captive-bred golden lion tamarin monkeys to the Brazilian jungle rang up a price tag of approximately $1 million, or $22,000 per surviving animal. Indeed, the reintroduced tamarins had borne ninety-seven offspring, by which measure the project was deemed a success, but to some the cost was excessive.

Others have wondered if money spent on captive breeding could be better spent on saving wild survivors. Ullas

A U.S. Fish and Wildlife worker with a sedated gray wolf planned for reintroduction to the wild. Reintroduction of wolves into Yellowstone National Park is highly controversial.

Karanth, a biologist with the Centre for Wildlife Studies in India, calculated that it would cost $150,000 to reintroduce 12 lion-tailed macaques to the wild. Alternatively, for just $30,000 per year, fifty guards could be employed to protect enough existing habitat for 250 to 300 monkeys.

Captive breeding and reintroduction programs have not been without controversy. In the early 1990s, farmers and ranchers in the western United States were outraged over a plan to reintroduce wolves to Yellowstone National Park. The ranchers predicted that the animals would leave the park boundaries and kill their livestock, despite assurances that wolves kill less than 1 percent of the livestock available to them.

By the spring of 1997, fifty-two wolves were living in Yellowstone and seemed to have become established in their new home. But according to local residents, the wolves have wandered outside of the park and gotten into scraps with humans. In October 1995 a man who killed a Yellowstone wolf in southern Montana was sentenced to six months in jail and fined $10,000. Opponents of the reintroduction program considered his action heroic.

Captive breeding programs raise troubling questions for saving endangered species. Some people feel that captive breeding artificially tampers with a species that nature has determined should become extinct. Nature, they feel, should be allowed to take its course; to them, captive breeding goes beyond people helping a species survive to people actually interfering with the natural order. Another criticism is that, since humanity caused the conditions that made a species become endangered, captive breeding is something that people do to make themselves feel better rather than something that is done for the good of a species. Since a growing number of species seem dependent on captive breeding in order to survive, these questions will continue to circulate.

Sources of refuge

As habitat for species continues to disappear throughout the world, the importance of national parks, wildlife refuges, and other protected natural areas becomes more and more critical.

In the United States, the National Wildlife Refuge System begun by Theodore Roosevelt in 1903 provides habitat for 240 threatened and endangered species on over 400 refuges. Today this system encompasses over 92 million acres.

Countries around the world have set aside land to help preserve species. The natural habitat of the Cuban crocodile, which lives only in swampland in central Cuba, was declared a sanctuary by the Cuban government. The African nation of Ethiopia made a national park out of the last remaining habitat of the walia ibex, a member of the goat family. In New Zealand, the takahe, a rare, flightless bird once thought to be extinct, lives in a protected area of the mountainous Lake District of South Island.

An important ally in the fight to save habitat for endangered species has been zoos. Assuming this role is another milestone in the continuing evolution of zoos, originally designed merely as places to display animals in concrete and steel cages. In the 1960s, as the first alarms were being raised about species extinction, zoos shifted their focus to captive breeding. Landscaped areas with moats and greenery replaced cages, and zoos became "arks"—safe places where endangered species could be bred and held until they could be released back into the wild.

However, as time went by, and more and more species were threatened, the ark began to get crowded. Realizing that they would soon be bursting at the seams with animals for which there was no safe place in the world, zoos redefined their mission to focus on field conservation, education, and research.

"Zoos are becoming protectors rather than collectors of wildlife," says Michael Hutchins, director for conservation

A giant panda relaxes in its zoo enclosure. Modern zoos take an active role in captive breeding, reintroduction, habitat protection, and conservation research to save endangered species.

and science at the American Zoo and Aquarium Association, in an article in *International Wildlife* magazine.

Many zoos are assisting efforts to protect species habitat. For example, money earned from the sale of rubber snakes at the Fort Worth Zoo in Texas (about $14,000 annually) goes to help protect a Peruvian rain forest. The Cincinnati Zoo's Conservation Fund is used to support endangered habitats across the globe. Some zoos "adopt" habitat regions in other lands, working with local authorities to improve management and protection while providing funding for equipment and other necessities. The Minnesota Zoo has adopted Ujung Kulon National Park in Java, home to the last remaining Javan rhinos, while the Wildlife Conservation Society, which operates several New York zoos, supports Amboseli National Park in Kenya.

While zoos will continue selective captive breeding programs, their emphasis is shifting toward species and habitat protection in the wild. Exhibits that stress these efforts help drive the message home to millions of zoo visitors each year.

"The collective impact of zoo involvement in the conservation of biodiversity could be enormous," says Hutchins. "Worldwide, some 1,000 zoos attract 600 million visitors—nearly 10 percent of the world's population."

Zoos are another ally in the race against extinction, a race that grows more critical with each passing day. Such tools as habitat preservation, captive breeding, wildlife refuges, and antihunting laws have helped the effort to save endangered species. However, there are growing concerns that these tools will not be enough.

5

This Land Is
Whose Land?

FLESH-EATING BEETLE BLOCKING HIGHWAY.

THIS FRONT-PAGE HEADLINE in the October 7, 1990, *Tulsa World* certainly was an eye-catcher. The accompanying article described the route of a proposed highway in Oklahoma that threatened the habitat of an endangered species known as the American burying beetle. Construction of the road, which would have provided better and safer access to a hospital for local Choctaw residents, was canceled.

Eventually this situation was resolved to everyone's satisfaction: The beetle was found in other areas and the Oklahoma Department of Transportation was able to build the road. Yet the question the incident raised over whose concerns should take precedence, endangered species or people, has come up repeatedly since the passage of the Endangered Species Act and spawned hundreds of controversies.

The issue of land use is the primary axis on which the entire endangered species debate turns. As with any complicated issue, no clear-cut solution exists.

Backlash against the ESA

The U.S. Congress almost certainly did not anticipate the consequences of the passage of the ESA in 1973.

It is unlikely that representatives considered that the ESA would prevent a highway from being built, yet because

Reprinted by permission of Chuck Asay and Creators Syndicate.

the law is so broad, this is precisely what happened. All species are equal in the eyes of the law.

"They [members of Congress] weren't thinking about dung beetles [when they passed the ESA]," commented Lynn Greenwalt, former head of the Fish and Wildlife Service. "They were thinking of huge grizzly bears and bald eagles and stately monarchs of the air."

By making all species equally important, Congress unwittingly sparked a firestorm of controversy that has often eclipsed the benefits of the ESA. Endangered species ultimately were viewed as the enemy.

The ESA's restrictions against "taking" either a species or its habitat are extremely broad. They cover everything from a developer who wants to build two hundred homes to a person who wants to put up a fence around his yard. Thus, time and time again, the needs of people have clashed with the needs of species.

In their book *Noah's Choice,* Charles C. Mann and Mark L. Plummer describe going out to dinner with a uniformed biologist employed by the Florida Game and Freshwater Fish Department. The biologist refused to eat in a crowded restaurant, fearful that his uniform, which identified him as someone who works on behalf of endangered species, would cause a confrontation with resentful customers. The authors write: "It occurred to us that matters had gone awry. Something about the simple presence of someone associated with government-organized efforts to preserve wild areas attracted hostility from the very people who live there."

People versus endangered species

Several well-publicized examples have fueled this hostility. In one instance, a family-owned sawmill in New Mexico may go out of business because all logging on property owned by the federal government was halted due to the possible effects of logging on the Mexican spotted owl.

Construction of a medical center in California was delayed for years because of its possible impact on the Delhi Sands flower-loving fly. Lastly, a woman's home in California was destroyed by fire after she was prevented from building a firebreak because it would have damaged the burrows of the kangaroo rat.

These are just some of the many instances in which the ESA has adversely affected people. A story in the *San Diego Union-Tribune* described anger over the ESA: "Fearful of seeing their land thrown into limbo by the U.S. Fish and

Reprinted by permission of Chuck Asay and Creators Syndicate.

Wildlife Service, many property owners regard protected species with hostility. According to Terry Anderson, a PERC [Political Economy Research Center] senior associate, 'Some farmers shoot, shovel and shut up,' when they see an endangered species on their land."

Some members of Congress and others want to change the ESA to make it less broad and more responsive to individual situations. In May 1997, California senator Dianne Feinstein said, "The Endangered Species Act—when it comes to the protection of life and property—really needs a second look. When it comes to a garter snake versus somebody's home and property and life and limb, I really think we need to get our priorities straight."

Congress is not the only organization that wants to reform the ESA. Feinstein's view is echoed by others who believe the ESA should make judgments about which species is most important. Certainly, they feel, grizzly bears and bald eagles should be saved, but efforts to save insects, plants, and fungi, especially when people are adversely affected, should not be aggressively pursued.

Biologists and other scientists, however, argue that the ESA has its priorities exactly right, because it does not make distinctions between species. All living things, no matter how small or insignificant they may seem, are part of the larger whole of plants, animals, algae, fungi, and bacteria that make up life on earth. Each species contributes in some manner to earth's biodiversity. In addition, it is difficult to determine which species to save. One criterion is whether a species may potentially benefit humans.

Saving plants, for example, could be very important. According to Peter H. Raven, director of the Missouri Botanical Garden in St. Louis, approximately 90 percent of the calories consumed by humans are supplied by about one

California senator Dianne Feinstein asserted that the ESA should be revised to consider the rights of property owners as well as those of the endangered species.

hundred kinds of plants. Tens of thousands of plant species currently exist on earth, and it is conceivable that someday humanity might have to turn to others for new sources of nourishment. In addition, plants supply ingredients used in more than one hundred drugs available today.

"Useful" species

In years past, the yew tree, found in the northwestern United States, was routinely logged. In the 1980s, however, scientists discovered that bark from the yew tree contained a chemical that was effective in treating certain types of cancer. But so many trees had been cut down that it was uncertain whether enough remained to produce adequate amounts of the chemical.

Plants can also aid humanity in other ways. In the late 1970s, a disease called grassy stunt virus that was spread by brown hopper insects threatened the rice crop in southern and eastern Asia. Scientists at the International Rice Research Institute in the Philippine Islands began a desperate search for a gene to resist the disease. After analyzing forty-seven thousand different varieties of plants, they finally found a resistant gene in one species of wild plant from a valley in India. Today, however, the valley has been flooded by a new hydroelectric project; if those scientists had been looking for that plant today they would not have found it.

Other less popular species may help humans. Many medicines, drugs, and medical treatments have come from living things without the "species star power" of a tiger or an eagle. A natural anesthetic called hyaluronidase that enables leeches to suck blood painlessly has been found to help relieve high blood pressure in people following certain types of operations. Certainly, before this discovery, no one ever considered a leech an "important" species.

Besides providing medicine and food, species help maintain the earth's life-sustaining balance in other ways. Clams and mussels act as natural cleaning filters, which help keep both freshwater and saltwater waterways clean. African elephants dig holes in riverbeds during droughts, making precious water available to many other creatures.

These are just a few of the many ways in which species aid the existence of life on earth. Undoubtedly many more have yet to be discovered; this is why some say it is senseless to take actions that may destroy any species before its role is understood.

"If the [living world], in the course of eons, has built something we like but do not understand," argues the naturalist Aldo Leopold, "then who but a fool would discard seemingly useless parts?"

Still, the notion of "rating" a species by its perceived worth to humans is extremely subjective. Some scientists critique the philosophy as arrogant. They contend that the mere fact that a species has existed for a long time gives it the right to continue to exist. Ecologist David Ehrenfeld, quoted in *Noah's Choice*, asserts, "Long-standing existence in Nature is deemed to carry with it the unimpeachable right to continued existence."

However, this right to continued existence is becoming dependent on whether a middle ground can be found between the needs of people and the needs of species.

Seeking middle ground

Considering the battles that have erupted over the incompatible needs of people and endangered species, it may be surprising to learn that these situations can sometimes end beneficially for both sides.

One such occasion was the clash in the American Northwest over the northern spotted owl. In June 1990, the Fish and Wildlife Service (FWS) declared the owl a threatened species and placed it on the endangered species list. A dark brown bird with white spots on the head and hindneck, the spotted owl is found in forests along the Pacific coast from southwestern British Columbia to southern California. The owl lives in the broken tops of trees, mostly in old-growth forests. Old-growth forests include trees that are at least two hundred years old. Each pair of spotted owls requires a large area for hunting and foraging, between four thousand and nine thousand acres.

Old-growth forests, however, are valuable to the timber industry because harvesting old trees yields the most wood. The result is that the owl's habitat has been reduced by 60 percent since 1800, according to a report issued in 1990 by the Interagency Scientific Committee.

In January 1992, the FWS designated 6.9 million acres of federal forest as critical to the owl's survival. Since this meant that logging was banned from a large amount of land, some claimed that the FWS ruling was tantamount to destroying the Northwest's timber industry.

The spotted owl was thus placed in the middle of a raging controversy between environmentalists and the timber industry. Logging communities throughout the Northwest braced for what they were certain would be economic devastation, as timber companies laid off workers in anticipation of work stoppages. People wore T-shirts displaying antienvironmentalist slogans—"Save a Logger—Eat an Owl" and "Loggers Are an Endangered Species"—as resentment mounted against the bird and the entire endangered species program. President George Bush, campaigning in the Northwest in 1992, summed up the feelings of many in the area by saying, "We'll be up to our neck in owls, and every millworker will be out of a job."

Fagan, for Associated Features. Used with permission.

Fortunately, these dire predictions did not come true. Logging jobs were indeed lost; *National Geographic* magazine estimated a loss of about 30,000 jobs between 1988 and 1995 in the entire Northwest region of Washington, Oregon, Idaho, and Montana. Logging jobs had already been declining, however, due to labor-saving devices, as well as the increasing practice of shipping logs to other countries to be milled.

Fortunately, other industries, primarily high-tech and electronics, moved into the Northwest and filled the gap left by logging. Although Oregon lost fifteen thousand jobs in forest products between 1989 and 1994, it gained almost twenty thousand jobs in high technology. By early 1995, technology jobs surpassed timber as the leading source of jobs in the state. Many former mill-workers were retrained for these positions, dispelling fears that workers would be forced into unemployment or minimum-wage jobs. In Springfield, Oregon, a new factory that will make compact discs could employ as many as fifteen hundred people at salaries starting at over $30,000 per year.

The spotted owl embroiled the Pacific Northwest in a bitter debate over the endangered species' right to live in the forests and the right of loggers to earn a living.

In the March 1997 issue of *National Geographic,* John G. Mitchell writes about the Oregon logging community of Sweet Home, for which economic disaster was predicted when the FWS restrictions were first announced. As Mitchell discovered, things had turned around for the town:

> I had seen it six years earlier when it was down on its luck and looking a bit dowdy around the edges. Now fresh paint glistened on storefronts. Newcomer businesses were in place: an electronics firm, a manufacturer of titanium golf-club heads, a maker of prefabricated wall units, a hairstyling salon.

Other factors have also helped the Northwest bounce back. Chief among these was the Pacific Northwest Forest

Plan, unveiled by the federal government in April 1994 as a solution to the spotted owl situation. Under the plan, more than 16 million acres of old-growth forest was set aside for the bird, while 5.5 acres were reopened for logging. In addition, the plan called for $1.2 billion in financial aid for the region to help the people and communities cope with the impact of the loss of so many acres to preservation.

The resolution of the spotted owl situation illustrated that the needs of people and endangered species do not always have to be at odds. The same holds true in other parts of the world as well.

A win-win situation

In the African nation of Zimbabwe, a program called CAMPFIRE (Communal Areas Management Programme for Indigenous Resources) uses financial incentives to discourage people from hunting endangered animals. Under the program, the central government grants authority over the wildlife in a region to local residents. Profits derived from maintaining the endangered animal and its habitat benefit the residents. For example, if a company builds facilities in the area for tourists who want to observe animals, most of the money generated by the venture goes to the local people, not the Zimbabwe central government. The residents can then allocate it as they see fit, such as to reimburse farmers who have lost crops to animals. One year, the village of Masoka used its share of the profits to build a school and health clinic, construct fences around people's fields to keep the animals out, and hire more game guards. Some villagers even turned over some of their grazing land to the animals to keep them healthy.

Unfortunately, this type of win-win situation for both people and endangered species is all too rare. Usually the endangered species comes out the loser. Then, drastic action is often necessary to stop extinction from claiming another victim.

6

The Future: Compromise or Chaos?

"MEN ARE EASILY inspired by human ideas, but they forget them again just as quickly. Only Nature is eternal, unless we senselessly destroy it. In fifty years' time nobody will be interested in the results of the conferences which fill today's headlines. But when, fifty years from now, a lion walks into the red dawn and roars resoundingly, it will mean something to people and quicken their hearts."

These words, written by African conservationist Bernhard Grzimke in 1959, are still relevant today. Grzimke was making a plea for the preservation of African wildlife, hoping that future generations would be able to enjoy the sheer pleasure of seeing such creatures in their natural environment.

Whether Grzimke's plea will be honored is uncertain. Many species, not just in Africa but all over the world, are rapidly approaching a point beyond which it may be impossible to save them. Extinction of hundreds, even thousands, of species could occur soon.

Extinction crisis: fact or fiction?

There is much debate about what the future holds for endangered species. Some scientists fear that the earth is hurtling toward an extinction crisis without precedent, a "time of great dying" in which thousands of species will be

Reprinted by permission of Kirk Anderson.

sucked down a vortex of mass destruction and vanish forever. The reason for such an extinction is that human activities (development, pollution, hunting, etc.) are causing the extinction rate to dramatically accelerate. Instead of losing between ten and one hundred species a year, the earth is losing tens of thousands each year. Others dispute this notion, saying there is little hard evidence to back up such alarming claims.

The "extinction crisis" received widespread publicity in 1980, when a study sponsored by the U.S. Council on Environmental Quality called *Global 2000 Report to the President* provided a grim view of the loss of species between the years 1980 and 2000. "Hundreds of thousands of species—perhaps as many as 20 percent of all species on earth—will be irretrievably lost as their habitats vanish, especially in tropical forests," the study concluded.

In 1979, Norman Myers offered his own sobering analysis of species extinction in his book *The Sinking Ark:*

> Let us suppose that . . . the final one-quarter of this century witnesses the elimination of 1 million species—a far from unlikely prospect. This would work out, during the course of 25 years, to an average extinction rate of 40,000 species per year, or rather over 100 species per day.

Since Myers wrote his book, the prospects for endangered species remain unclear. Some continue to warn of a major extinction event looming on the horizon. Harvard

University professor Edward O. Wilson calculates that the earth is losing thirty thousand species per year, a rate 120,000 times the natural background rate of the prehistoric past. Four years later, the World Conservation Union of Cambridge, England, which has been tracking threatened wildlife for thirty years, concluded that 34 percent of fish, 25 percent of amphibians, 25 percent of mammals, 20 percent of reptiles, and 11 percent of birds were threatened with extinction.

However, clouding the issue is the fact that no one really knows how many species exist on earth; estimates range from 10 million to 100 million, and scientists are constantly discovering new species. In the early 1990s, a new species of salamander was discovered in California's densely populated Los Angeles County. Seven new species of monkeys have been discovered in Brazil since 1990.

It is this uncertainty about numbers and statistics, and what they may (or may not) mean, that has made it so difficult to get a firm grip on future extinction rates.

"There are frequent statements that hundreds of species are going extinct every year," says John Terborgh, a biologist at Duke University in North Carolina quoted in "Life on the Brink" by Karen Schmidt. "It may be true, but we have no evidence—it's just hand-waving."

Statistical difficulties

Further complicating matters is the difficulty of declaring a species extinct. The example of the passenger pigeon, whose extinction was known to the precise day, is extremely rare; more often scientists have to rely on unsubstantiated secondary information to determine whether extinction has occurred.

"Rumors of sightings [of species thought to be extinct] leak out for decades because there are thousands of hopeful people," says Terborgh. "Even in extremely well-studied groups of organisms, such as birds, it takes decades to document extinction."

Even when extinction seems certain, events have proven otherwise. The coelacanth is a fish thought to be extinct for millions of years. Yet in 1939 a coelacanth was caught off the coast of South Africa. Since then, coelacanths have also been found off the Madagascar coast.

More recently, in January 1998, researchers in India photographed a rare Blewitt's owl, previously considered extinct because its last confirmed sighting was in 1884.

Another difficulty for those trying to track species extinction is that data for a particular species doesn't necessarily apply to others. An extinction rate for reptiles cannot be applied to birds, mammals, or plants.

"Different groups in different areas are punished to different degrees—a single number can't capture what is going on," says David Jablonski, a paleontologist at the University of Chicago quoted in "Life on the Brink."

Hopeful signs

But despite the uncertainty over numbers, one thing that most researchers can agree upon is that the rate of extinction is increasing, primarily because of human activity. This has prompted the realization that even while the debate continues over extinction, action has to be taken now to save species at risk.

Fortunately, the future for endangered species may not be as bleak as once believed.

In Peru, troops that once fought military engagements are now used to combat poaching of the endangered vicuña, a cousin of the llama that in the early 1990s had been reduced by wanton killing to less than fifty thousand

Coelacanths were believed extinct for millions of years until they were rediscovered near South Africa and Madagascar in the twentieth century.

in number. Today, however, vicuña populations have nearly doubled, and the animal is leading an economic renaissance for Peruvian mountain villages. Reviving an ancient Incan tradition called the *Chaku,* villagers form a mile-long human chain to corral the animals and shear their wool, which they then trade to the government for needed economic improvements for their communities.

There is also hope for the whooping crane, long the subject of efforts to increase its meager population. In October 1997 a flock of the endangered birds followed a group of ultralight planes on an experimental flight from Idaho to the Bosque del Apache National Wildlife Refuge in New Mexico. The goal was for the birds to establish a new winter nesting site in addition to their Aransas refuge, so that the entire U.S. population of whoopers wouldn't be grouped in one location. If the experiment succeeds (preliminary indications are encouraging), researchers hope to use the ultralight planes to introduce a new migratory flock of whoopers to the southeastern United States, a region from which the birds vanished decades ago.

A vicuña in the Andes Mountains of Peru. The Peruvian military protects the vicuña, improving the vitality of the species and in turn benefiting the villagers' economy.

New research techniques are also offering hope for species in peril. U.S. scientists have begun using satellites to track endangered animals; this enables them to follow the movements of whales, seals, tuna, and other creatures that can't be accurately tracked with radio transmitters over vast oceans.

By implanting sensors that record seals' vital signs and transmit that information to satellites, scientists are discovering information that may one day help them preserve species, such as how the seals can hold their breath during hour-long dives. (Indications are that they store oxygen-rich red blood cells in their spleen before diving.) They are also learning more about the lifestyles of migratory creatures, such as the peregrine falcon, which flies from the Arctic to South America. By monitoring where the falcon stops during its long flights, researchers can pinpoint which habitat areas need protection.

Hope can also be found in the success of the wolf reintroduction program at Yellowstone National Park. The wolves have become a big tourist attraction, boosting the local economy by an estimated $23 million yearly. Each wolf wears a special collar that sends out a radio signal, so workers can track and retrieve any that wander off park lands. A group called Defenders of Wildlife has begun paying ranchers for any livestock that wolves kill. These positive solutions hold the promise that similar methods can perhaps be applied to other reintroduction programs.

Early in 1997 scientists at the Roslin Institute near Edinburgh, Scotland, startled the world by revealing that they had successfully cloned a female sheep. Although cloning technology is still in its infancy, one day it may be possible to produce exact copies of endangered life forms in order to perpetuate the species and thwart extinction.

The wolf reintroduction program in Yellowstone Park has been a success for both the wolves and the local residents.

Revising government policy

There is even hopeful news in the sometimes raucous debate over the Endangered Species Act. Efforts to make the ESA less onerous to property owners have resulted in an FWS concept called a Habitat Conservation Plan (HCP). An HCP allows a project to go forward within the habitat of an endangered or threatened species, and even permits the "taking" of some members of the species. In exchange, the responsible party must devise a plan to improve the species' overall chances of survival, often by strengthening habitat elsewhere. The principle behind the HCP is compromise: projects are built *and* habitat is protected.

Having observed the ESA in action since 1973, many environmentalists now realize that instead of trying to aid species on an individual basis, it would be more effective to preserve entire ecosystems, treating both habitats and the species that live within them as the "organism" at risk.

Saving ecosystems was the idea behind the 1993 establishment of the National Biological Service within the U.S. Department of the Interior. The purpose of this agency is to assess the status of all U.S. ecosystems and the biodiversity found within them. By keeping track of ecosystems, it is hoped that threats to species will become apparent early, reducing the need for emergency measures later.

Although each day brings new reports of species in peril, enough positive developments have occurred to shed some rays of hope on the future for endangered species.

Are humans endangering themselves?

A 1992 *Buffalo News* editorial cartoon shows two chatting cockroaches on a blank page. "Well, people succeeded in reducing biodiversity down to one species," says one cockroach to the other. "And they always thought it would be them."

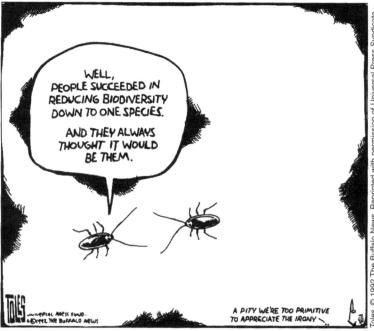

Toles. © 1992 The Buffalo News. Reprinted with permission of Universal Press Syndicate. All rights reserved.

The cartoon humorously illustrates the possibility that by pushing so many species toward extinction, humanity may ultimately be forcing itself down that same dead-end road. A world in which thousands of species have been wiped out might be a world that cannot support human life, or perhaps a world in which people would not want to live.

"We don't want to experience a K-T scale extinction event," contends David Jablonski, referring to the mass extinction that occurred at the end of the Cretaceous period, when approximately 70 percent of all life on earth vanished. "In the blackest scenario, we could be driving ourselves toward a world of rats, weeds and cockroaches."

"Ultimately, we are the endangered species," said Senator Patrick Leahy in 1978:

> *Homo sapiens* is perceived to stand at the top of the pyramid of life, but the pinnacle is a precarious station. We need a large measure of self-consciousness to constantly remind us of the commanding role which we enjoy only at the favor of the web of life that sustains us.

The knowledge that species preservation is not only important but necessary is approximately one hundred years old. During that time, people's thinking has changed dramatically, from perceiving an inexhaustible supply of plants and animals to realizing that measures must be taken to safeguard the preservation of species, even though those measures sometimes impact on human activity. In the coming years, the ability to balance the needs of species as well as the needs of humanity will determine the future course of life on earth.

Organizations to Contact

CITES Secretariat
15 chemin des Anemones
Case Postale 456
CH-1219 Chatelaine
Geneva, Switzerland
(+4122) 9799139140

CITES is an international treaty that protects wildlife against overexploitation. The treaty monitors international trade to prevent it from threatening species with extinction.

Environmental Defense Fund (EDF)
257 Park Ave. South
New York, NY 10010
(212) 505-2100

The EDF was founded in 1967 by volunteer conservationists on Long Island (New York) to promote a ban on the pesticide DDT. Today the EDF has more than 300,000 members and tackles a broad range of environmental issues.

National Audubon Society
700 Broadway
New York, NY 10003
(212) 979-3000

The society was founded in 1905 and named for the famous ornithologist and wildlife artist John James Audubon. Currently, it has over 550,000 members. Its mission is to conserve and restore natural ecosystems, focusing on birds and other wildlife, for the benefit of humanity and the earth's biological diversity.

National Endangered Species Act Reform Coalition
1050 Thomas Jefferson St. NW, Seventh Floor
Washington, DC 20007
(202) 333-7481

The coalition is composed of groups that champion the rights of farmers, ranchers, water and power companies, and others. The group's goal is to reform the Endangered Species Act. In particular, it wants to minimize the ESA's impact on private landowners and reduce the federal government's role in the management of species.

Sierra Club
85 Second St., Second Floor
San Francisco, CA 94105-3441
(415) 977-5500

The club was founded in 1892 by naturalist John Muir. It is a nonprofit, member-supported organization that promotes conservation of the natural environment. It is divided into sixty-five chapters covering the United States and Canada.

U.S. Fish and Wildlife Service
4401 North Fairfax Dr., Room 452
Arlington, VA 22203
(703) 358-2171

A bureau of the U.S. Department of the Interior, the Division of Endangered Species has the primary responsibility for administering the Endangered Species Act.

World Wildlife Fund (WWF)
1250 24th St. NW
Washington, DC 20037
(202) 293-4800

The World Wildlife Fund is part of the international WWF network, which has national organizations or representatives in more than fifty countries. The WWF is a leader in worldwide efforts to protect the world's threatened wildlife and the habitats they need to survive.

Suggestions for Further Reading

Norman D. Anderson and Walter R. Brown, *Lemurs.* New York: Dodd, Mead & Company, 1984.

Caroline Arnold, *Rhino.* New York: Morrow Junior Books, 1995.

"The Call of the Wild," *Time for Kids,* February 7, 1997.

Susan DeStefano, *Theodore Roosevelt: Conservation President.* New York: Twenty-First Century Books, 1993.

Jon Erickson, *Dying Planet: The Extinction of Species.* Blue Ridge Summit, PA: TAB Books, 1991.

Roger Few, *Macmillan Children's Guide to Endangered Animals.* New York: Macmillan, 1993.

Dorothy Hinshaw Patent, *The Whooping Crane: A Comeback Story.* New York: Clarion Books, 1988.

Science Year 1996: The World Book Annual Science Supplement. Chicago: World Book, 1995.

Sally Tolan, *John Muir.* Milwaukee, WI: Gareth Stevens Children's Books, 1990.

Lois Warburton, *Rainforests.* San Diego: Lucent Books, 1990.

Works Consulted

Books and Periodicals

Thomas B. Allen, *Vanishing Wildlife of North America.* Washington, DC: National Geographic Society, 1974.

Bruce E. Beans, *Eagle's Plume.* New York: Scribner, 1996.

Raymond Bonner, *At the Hand of Man: Peril and Hope for African Wildlife.* New York: Knopf, 1993.

Douglas H. Chadwick and Joel Sartore, *The Company We Keep.* Washington, DC: National Geographic Society, 1995.

David A. Dary, *The Buffalo Book.* Chicago: Sage, 1974.

John Fleischman, "Mass Extinctions Come to Ohio," *Discover,* June 1997.

John Ripley Forbes, *In the Steps of the Great American Zoologist William Temple Hornaday.* New York: M. Evans, 1966.

Warren Getler, "The Polar Bear Slides," *Audubon,* May/June 1997.

R. J. Hoage, *Animal Extinctions: What Everyone Should Know.* Washington, DC: Smithsonian Institution Press, 1985.

Christopher Joyce, "Working to Keep Extinction at Bay," *USA Weekend,* June 27–29, 1997.

Charles C. Mann and Mark L. Plummer, *Noah's Choice: The Future of Endangered Species.* New York: Knopf, 1995.

John G. Mitchell, "In the Line of Fire: Our National Forests," *National Geographic*, March 1997.

Matt Moffett, "Once They Chased Guerrillas, but This Is a Different Animal," *Wall Street Journal,* June 13, 1997.

Jay Monaghan, *The Book of the American West.* New York: Julian Messner, 1963.

Norman Myers, *The Primary Source.* New York: W. W. Norton, 1984.

Norman Myers, *The Sinking Ark.* Oxford: Pergamon Press, 1979.

Norman Myers and Julian L. Simon, *Scarcity or Abundance?* New York: W. W. Norton, 1994.

Madeleine J. Nash, "The Age of Cloning," *Time,* March 10, 1997.

Charles Norman, *John Muir.* New York: Julian Messner, 1957.

Steve Pollock, *The Atlas of Endangered Animals.* New York: Facts On File, 1993.

David M. Raup, *Extinction: Bad Genes or Bad Luck?* New York: W. W. Norton, 1991.

Karen Schmidt, "Life on the Brink," *Earth,* April 1997.

Jack Denton Scott, *Return of the Buffalo.* New York: G. P. Putnam's Sons, 1976.

Les Sillars, "First Wolves, Now Bears," *Alberta Report,* May 19, 1997.

Brenda Stalcup, ed., *Endangered Species: Opposing Viewpoints.* San Diego: Greenhaven Press, 1996.

Darryl Stewart, *From the Edge of Extinction.* New York: Methuen, 1978.

Fiona Sunquist, "End of the Ark?" *International Wildlife,* November/December 1995.

Courtenay Thompson, "Indian Tribe Will Revive Whaling," *Newhouse News Service,* October 26, 1997.

John F. Turner, *The Magnificent Bald Eagle.* New York: Random House, 1971.

Donovan Webster, "The Looting and Smuggling and Fencing and Hoarding of Impossibly Precious, Feathered and Scaly Wild Things," *New York Times Magazine,* February 16, 1997.

Internet Sources

"Animal Bytes: Bald Eagle," December 1996. Sea World/ Busch Gardens. Available www.seaworld.org/animal_bytes/ bald_eagleab.html

Ron Arnold and Alan Gottlieb, "The Endangered Species Act: In Need of Change." The Endangered Species Act Needs Change. Available www.cdfe.org/endanger.html

"Attwater's Greater Prairie Chicken—*Tympanuchus Cupido Attwateri.*" Environmental Impact on Endangered Animals. Available ananke.advanced.org/2878/tx_attwater's_ greater_prairie_chicken.html

"Attwater's Prairie Chickens Continue to Decline in Wild; Captive Birds Increase, Ready for Release into Wild This Year," May 17, 1995. Available sturgeon.irml.r2.fws.gov/ news-rel/apc

"Bald Eagle's Dramatic Recovery Takes It Off Critical List," September 1994. EDF Letter. Available www.edf.org/pubs/ EDF-Letter/1994/Sep/a_baldeagle.html

"Black Rhino." Lincoln Park Zoo. Available www.lpzoo.com/animals/mammals/brhino.html

"Box Score," October 31, 1998. U.S. Fish and Wildlife
Service, Division of Endangered Species. Available
www.fws.gov/r9endspp/boxscore.html

Bill Dawson, "Prairie Chicken's Numbers Up to 58,"
Houston Chronicle, April 7, 1997. Available
www.zooweb.net/atc/houcron.htm

"Digest of Federal Resource Laws of Interest to the U.S.
Fish and Wildlife Service." U.S. Fish and Wildlife Service,
Division of Endangered Species. Available www.fws.gov/
laws/digest/reslaws/migtrea.html

David Ehrlinger, "The Eightieth Anniversary of the Death of
the Last Passenger Pigeon," September 1994. Cincinnati
Zoo and Botanical Garden: World of Wonder. Available
www.cincyzoo.org/zoo_visit/pigeon.html

"Elephants and Ivory." WWF International. Available
www.panda.org/ resources/factsheets/species/33eleph.htm

"Endangered Species," October 1996. U.S. Fish and Wildlife
Service, Division of Endangered Species. Available
www.fws.gov/r9endspp/esasum.html

"Endangered Species Act Forum," July 19, 1996. John F.
Kennedy School of Government, Harvard University.
Available ksgwww.harvard.edu/~ksgpress/upendang.htm

"Endangered Species General Statistics," May 31, 1997.
U.S. Fish and Wildlife Service, Division of Endangered
Species. Available www.fws.gov/r9endspp/esastats.html

"Fact Sheet: Bald Eagle." Sea World/Busch Gardens.
Available www.seaworld.org/animal_bytes/eaglefc.html

John Flesher, "Traditional Foes Unite to Save Endangered
Bird." Associated Press. Available www.kirtland.cc.mi.us/
honors/warbler.htm

"Giant Panda, Endangered." World Wildlife Fund Canada.
Available www.wwfcanada.org/facts/panda.html

"Great Auk (*Pinguinus impennis*)." Available www-nais.CCRS.NRCAN.gc.ca/schoolnet/issues/risk/birds/ebirds/grtauk.html

"A Guide to the Laws and Treaties of the United States for Protecting Migratory Birds." U.S. Fish and Wildlife Service, Division of Endangered Species. Available www.fws.gov/r9mbmo/intrnltr/treatlaw.html#lacey

"History of the CITES Treaty Regime." Available moby.ucdavis.edu/GAWS/122/2alfa/jhistory.htm

"Legislative History of the Endangered Species Act." National Endangered Species Act Reform Coalition. Available www.nesarc.org/endang.htm

"Marine Mammal Protection Act of 1972," November 11, 1996. Office of Protected Resources Home Page. Available www.nmfs.gov/tmcintyr/mmpahome.html

"Mountain Gorilla, Endangered." World Wildlife Fund Canada. Available www.wwfcanada.org/facts/mtngorla.html

"National Endangered Species Act Reform Coalition," February 5, 1997. National Endangered Species Act Reform Coalition. Available www.nesarc.org

"Northern Spotted Owl." Northwest Forestry Association—Forest Friends & Foes. Available www.nwtrees.org/spotowl1.htm

"North Pacific Fur Seal Conservation Efforts." North Pacific Fur Seal Depleted Species Home Page. Available www.nmfs.gov/tmcintyr/depleted/frsealre.html

"OEPA Environmental Law Summary: Marine Mammal Protection Act," February 20, 1997. DOE Office of Environmental Policy and Assistance. Available tis-nt.eh.doe.gov/oepa/law_sum/MMPA.HTM

"The Passenger Pigeon—Gone from the Face of the Earth." Available www.ris.net/~tony/ppigeon.html

"President's Forest Plan: The Gridlock Continues." The National Forestry Association. Available www.woodcom.com/woodcom/nfa/nfabp06.html

"Recovery Status." Oil Spill Public Information Center. Available www.alaska.net/~ospic/recover.html

"Rhino Information." The International Rhino Foundation. Available www.rhinos-irf.org/rhinos/

"Sierra Club Fact Sheet on John Muir," March 1993. Sierra Club. Available www.sierraclub.org/john_muir_exhibit/life/fact_sheet_on_john_muir_by_the_sierra_club.html

"Spotted Owl, Endangered." World Wildlife Fund Canada. Available www.wwfcanada.org/facts/spotdowl.html

"Spotted Owl/Old Growth Forests." Newton's Apple. Available ericir.syr.edu/Projects/Newton/11/oldgrwth.html

"The Student CITES Project, 1997." The Student CITES Project 1997. Available www.studentcites.org/visitor/visitor.htm

"TRAFFIC East/Southern Africa." WWF International. Available www.panda.org/kids/portfoli/traffic/page6.htm

"Treaties." Treaties. Available www.conservationtreaty.org/cites.html

"The Truth About the Spotted Owl." California Forests Online. Available www.foresthealth.org/owl1.html

Richard L. Wallace, "Why Endangered Species Protection vs. Economic Development Doesn't Have to Be a Win-Lose Scenario." The Ethical Spectacle. Available www.spectacle.org/196/rich1.html

"What Are Some Basic Facts About the National Wildlife Refuge System?" April 5, 1996. America's National Wildlife Refuges. Available refuges.fws.gov/NWRSFiles/FAQs/FastFacts.html

"What Happened on March 24, 1989." Oil Spill Public Information Center. Available www.alaska.net/~ospic/rpln.html

"Whooping Crane, Endangered." World Wildlife Fund Canada. Available www.wwfcanada.org/facts/whopncrn.html

Index

Picture Credits

Cover photo: DigitalVision

Corbis-Bettmann, 47

DigitalVision, 7, 15, 16, 40

© Francois Gohier/Photo Researchers, Inc., 12, 72

Jim Harter, *Animals*, Dover Publications, Inc., 1979, 35, 36

© Fred W. Lahrman/Photo Researchers, Inc., 49

Library of Congress, 44, 45, 48

© Tom McHugh/Photo Researchers, Inc., 42, 71

Eric Miller/Impact Visuals, 39

North Wind Picture Archives, 38

Reuters/Corbis-Bettmann, 27, 62

© Michael Tweedie/Photo Researchers, Inc., 25

U.S. Fish and Wildlife Service, 20

U.S. Fish and Wildlife Service Photo by Bill Fitzpatrick, 19

U.S. Fish and Wildlife Service Photo by Gary Halvorsen, 50

U.S. Fish and Wildlife Service Photo by John and Karen Hollingsworth, 32, 66

U.S. Fish and Wildlife Service Photo by Dave Mech, 73

U.S. Fish and Wildlife Service Photo by Norm Nelson, 13

U.S. Fish and Wildlife Service Photo by Pedro Ramirez Jr., 55

U.S. Fish and Wildlife Service Photo by Ron Singer, 22

U.S. Fish and Wildlife Service Photo by Gary M. Stolz, 51, 57

U.S. Fish and Wildlife Service Photo by Ted Swem, 53

About the Author

Russell Roberts graduated from Rider University in Lawrenceville, New Jersey. A full-time freelance writer, he has published over 150 articles and short stories and four previous nonfiction books: *Stolen: The Stolen Base in Baseball, Down the Jersey Shore, Discover the Hidden New Jersey,* and *All About Blue Crabs and How to Catch Them.*

He currently resides in Bordentown, New Jersey, with his family and a lazy cat named Rusti.